Let's Learn About Healthy Eating

Margaret Collins

P·C·P

Paul Chapman
Publishing

Paul Chapman Publishing
A SAGE Publications Company
1 Oliver's Yard
55 City Road
London EC1Y 1SP

SAGE Publications Inc.
2455 Teller Road
Thousand Oaks, California 91320

SAGE Publications India Pvt Ltd.
B-42, Panchsheel Enclave
Post Box 4109
New Delhi 110 017

www.luckyduck.co.uk

Commissioning Editor: George Robinson
Editorial Team: Wendy Ogden, Sarah Lynch, Mel Maines
Designer: Nick Shearn
Illustrator: Philippa Drakeford

**A catalogue record for this book is available from the British Library
Library of Congress Control Number 2005937919**

ISBN13 978-1-4129-2253-1
ISBN10 1-4129-2253-4

Printed on paper from sustainable resources.

Printed in Great Britain by The Cromwell Press Ltd., Trowbridge, Wiltshire.

Acknowledgments

George Robinson who suggested a need for this book and lit my fire.

Jamie Oliver's School Dinners TV programme that fanned the flames!

Teachers everywhere who would like their children to be healthier!

Lucas for the fun vegetables poster.

Philippa for all her charming drawings.

How to use the CD-ROM

The CD-ROM contains a PDF file, labelled 'Let's Learn About Healthy Eating. pdf' which consists of worksheets for each lesson in this resource. You will need Acrobat Reader version 3 or higher to view and print these resources.

There are also pages that contain live links to each website mentioned in this book. You will need an active connection to the internet to utilise the live links. If you click on the link you wish to acces, it will open the page in your browser window.

To photocopy the worksheets directly from this book, set your photocopier to enlarge by 125% and align the edge of the page to be copied against the leading edge of the copier glass (usually indicated by an arrow).

Contents

Introduction

A balanced diet

The following is from *Teachers magazine* Nov. 2004 issue 35:

> The availability of junk food and the pernicious influences of child-targeted advertising, combined with a general trend for young people to be relatively inactive, is a recipe for disaster. A diminished life-expectancy and reduced quality of life for the unfit young have been predicted by experts, and unless things change, the loss of potential suffered by the nation could affect us all.

(See www.teachernet.gov.uk/teachers/issue35/primary/features/Balanceddiet)

Fit for school

The following is also from the above website.

In November 2004 Charles Clarke announced the *Healthy Living Blueprint for Schools* (www.apse.org.uk).

The *Healthy Living Blueprint for Schools* supports schools in working towards five key objectives:

1. To promote a school ethos and environment which encourages a healthy lifestyle

2. To use the full capacity and flexibility of the curriculum to achieve a healthy lifestyle

3. To ensure the food and drink available across the school day reinforces the healthy lifestyle message

4. To provide high-quality physical education and school sport and promote physical activity as part of a lifelong healthy lifestyle

5. To promote an understanding of the full range of issues and behaviours which will effect lifelong health.

A key theme of the blueprint is that good health and effective learning go hand-in-hand; a healthy body can lead to a healthy brain.

We need to change children's attitudes to food. This book seeks to help teachers to deliver a curriculum that encompasses numbers 1, 2, 3 and 5 of the above list and to help children to be 'fit for school'. A whole-school approach is recommended.

There is to be a new healthy schools category in this year's National Teaching Awards and according to new Ofsted guidelines, from September 2005 Her Majesty's Inspectors will be assessing the healthiness – or otherwise – of pupils' lifestyles (TES March 11 2005).

This programme of food related activities will be of particular value to schools who are working towards the healthy eating strand of the National Healthy Schools Standard.

> Promotion of food and drink high in fat, salt and/or sugar can negatively influence children's food choices and lead to an unhealthy diet…
> Page 15 *Healthy Living Blueprint for Schools* (ibid)
> (See fact sheets on fats, salt and sugar for more information).

There is a move towards healthy eating, not only because so many children are overweight, but because it is recognised that we are what we eat. Many children are eating too many of the foods that are not good for their health. Many are drinking too many of the sugary or high caffeine drinks that are not good for them. With moderation, all foods are good for us. It is only by drinking and eating too many of the foods that are not so good for us that health can suffer. It's a question of balance.

The *Healthy Living Blueprint* (ibid) stresses the importance of laying strong foundations for healthy lifestyles by promoting positive attitudes to health. This includes that all children have a nutritious, well-balanced diet, which is a key building block for learning, achievement and overall health and happiness. Spotlight, the *National Children's Bureau journal* states (issue 5, March 05) that:

> We must also support a culture change so that instead of being 'maverick' and unusual, being healthy is embraced as natural, attractive and fun. This need not mean never eating chocolate, crisps or sweets. Healthy, as NCB understands it, includes being able to choose unhealthy options occasionally in the context of a positive overall approach, understanding and attitude to health.

It is little wonder that children are eating unhealthy options or 'treats' foods and drinks far too often when the same issue of *Spotlight* goes on to say that:

> TV advertising is dominated by positive messages relating to the least healthy foods… The Food Commission has calculated that for every £1 spent by the World Health Organisation on promoting healthy diets, £500 is spent by the food industry on promoting the very foods that contribute to unhealthy diets.

The 'wartime' diet that was rich in vegetables, low in sugars, meat and fats resulted in a generation of people who were reasonably healthy. People of that generation were used to buying raw ingredients and making their food. Cakes were usually baked at home; some families ate home baked bread. Sandwiches were made with bread made from unrefined flour with margarine and scanty fillings. Main meals were cooked from raw meat and vegetables and pastry was home made.

Since supermarkets introduced so many ready-made foods that are high in sugars, salt, fat, additives and preservatives, many hardworking parents have used these time saving foods to feed their families. The manufacturers of these foods seem to be only concerned with producing tasty addictive foods that children will request. Their remit is not to produce nourishing foods that growing bodies need but rather to produce low cost foods using ingredients that may not all be of good quality. Profit is all!

In the past, school children learnt about nutrition and cooked meals at school. The national curriculum has taken 'cookery' or 'home economics' off the timetable in many secondary schools and few primary schools have time or facilities for children to do simple cooking. The pattern of eating ready-made foods spreads out into the community like wildfire and fewer and fewer people make meals from basic ingredients.

Many of our fast food outlets also provide tasty and addictive foods that children love. In moderation and for treats, these foods will do children little harm. However, if a child's diet is composed totally of these foods there is room for doubt about the body's ability to convert them into healthy body building blocks.

Robinson (2005) states in *Healthy Eating in Primary Schools* (Chapter Seven) that The World Health Organisation (Europe) have published dietary guidelines for children and young people aged seven to 18 years (WHO, 2005) and lists these as:

Twelve Steps to Healthy Eating for Children and Adolescents

1. Eat a nutritious diet based on a variety of foods originating mainly from plants rather than animals.

2. Eat bread, grains, pasta, rice or potatoes several times a day.

3. Eat a variety of vegetables and fruits, preferably fresh and local, several times a day.

4. Replace fatty meat and meat products with beans, legumes, lentils, fish, poultry or lean meat.

5. Use low fat milk and dairy products (kefir, sour milk, yoghurt and cheese) that are low in both fat and salt.

6. Control fat intake (not more than 30% of daily energy) and replace most saturated fats with unsaturated vegetable oils or soft margarines.

7. Select foods that are low in sugar, and eat refined sugar sparingly, limiting the frequency of sugary drinks and sweets.

8. Choose a low-salt diet. Total salt intake should be limited to 5 g. per day, including the salt in bread and processed, cured and preserved foods. (Salt iodisation should be universal where iodine deficienty is endemic.)

9. Prepare food in a safe and hygienic way. Steam, bake, boil or microwave to help reduce the amount of added fat.

10. Children and adolescents should continue to learn about the preparation of food and cooking processes.

11. Explain to children and adolescents the benefits of breast-feeding, compared with infant formula.

12. Encourage children and adolescents to learn to enjoy physical activity. Reduce 'non-active' time spent on TV, video, computer games and surfing the internet and maintain body weight between the recommended limits by taking moderate levels of physical activity daily.

The author also states that nutritionists have found an easy way for us to achieve a healthy balanced diet, called *The Balance of Good Health* (Food Standards Agency 2001). It is listed below.

The Balance of Good Health is based on the Government's guidelines for a healthy diet. These, with the exception of numbers 7 and 8, can be understood by even the youngest children in primary schools.

1. Base your meals on starchy foods.

2. Eat lots of fruit and veg.

3. Eat more fish – including a portion of oily fish each week.

4. Cut down on saturated fat and sugar.

5. Try to eat less salt – no more than 6 g a day for adults.

6. Get active and try to be a healthy weight.

7. Drink plenty of water.

8. Don't skip breakfast.

Let's widen children's understanding about foods

We need to make sure that all children realise that some foods are for treats. Treats are OK and we all like treats but if we only ever eat 'treat' foods our bodies will not grow up to be healthy bodies; we can become unhealthy as we get older. We need to make sure that children know about foods and drinks that are good for us and those that are treats. We need to remind children that fizzy drinks are OK for treats but that if they only ever drink fizzy drinks, and never drink water, their bodies may become unhealthy as they get older.

Many children are only happy to eat foods that they like and refuse to taste other foods. In schools where I worked in the 60s and 70s low cost meals were made from scratch in the school kitchens. The diet was varied and interesting; children were encouraged to, at least, taste everything on their plate even though they might prefer to eat all of some parts of the meal and leave others. There was no choice of menu. Things changed in the 80s as kitchens became redundant when school meals went out to contract. More and more children have been eating poor quality foods as a regular daily occurrence, and when they are presented with more nourishing foods they do not want to taste them. It is not only school meals; many restaurants also buy in pre-prepared foods to serve to their customers.

This cycle of eating too much of the wrong foods and too few of nourishing body-building foods needs to be addressed. In some areas of the country school meals organisers are trying out new menus and parents and teachers are finding out that children are less difficult and less hyperactive when eating them. With the government allocating more money for healthier school meals, many children previously not so well nourished will soon be healthier, but this change will take time to have an effect on children's bodies.

One thing we can do in schools is to talk about different foods and encourage children to experiment with new tastes and flavours. We can help them to learn about the production of foods; how foods are prepared and cooked. We also need to ensure that parents understand what we are doing and why; we need their support. While making sure that children know that no food is actually bad for them, they need to understand that it is possible to eat a poor diet. We can help them to understand that some foods are healthier for them than others and that foods that are not quite so healthy should be enjoyed as treats. We can help children to know that a balanced meal contains some fat, sugar and salt, but not too much.

'Fresh' and 'freshly'

These terms can mean different things to different people. In these activities 'fresh' means 'food that is raw, has not been processed, frozen or heated and contains no preservatives'.

'Freshly' refers to food that has been made recently; it may be used with 'baked' as in 'freshly baked'.

Eating disorders

One of the aims of this book is to make eating a more pleasurable activity for children. While helping children to be better informed, interested in and excited about food, what we don't want to do is to make children stressed or anxious about 'healthy eating' and worried about eating foods that are not particularly good for them. Though the word 'diet' has been used in this book meaning the food we eat, as in 'a healthy diet', 'a balanced diet'; the idea of 'dieting' has not been mentioned for that very reason.

How will you start?

You may want to start at once with a whole-school focus on healthy eating – perhaps as part of your Healthy Schools Standard programme. It may be that you prefer to start this work with the youngest children and follow it through as the children move through the school.

Inform parents and carers

The *Healthy Living Blueprint for Schools* (ibid) states on page 3:

> The partnership of home and school is critical in shaping how children and young people behave, particularly where health is concerned. Each must reinforce the other. This is not always easy, of course, but schools are well placed to lead by example.

However you decide to do it, it is vital that you inform parents that you are doing this work and perhaps try to involve them in these lessons. You'll need their cooperation! They need to know that you won't be criticising the food that they prepare for their children; it's just that we all know that some foods are better for us than others. You need to explain that what you will be doing is helping their children to understand that some foods provide good building blocks for their future health while other foods are not quite so good, especially if eaten all the time. Reassure parents that though we enjoy these 'not so healthy' foods, we will be trying to get children to understand these should be reserved for treats rather than everyday eating.

Feeding a family is one way that parents and carers show that they love their children. It would be very wrong to upset parents by suggesting that they are not feeding their children the right foods.

There are various ways of involving parents/carers. The topic can be introduced at the school's Annual Meeting and a letter to parents could inform them of how your school is going to do this. Individual class parents' meetings could help them to understand how they could help. There are suggested introductory letters on the following pages.

There is also a suggested letter to parents at the beginning of each section. This is to alert parents about the topic and to ask for their cooperation. It also invites any comments regarding children's allergies or special needs.

Can we help parents, through their children's activities, to recognise that they have a vital part to play? Can we help them to understand the importance of using fresh unprocessed ingredients wherever possible?

Looking for Innovation in Healthy School Meals (Nov 2004) states that:

> Pupils who eat meals made with fresh, unprocessed ingredients and who have access to drinking water have better concentration, improved attention spans, are less likely to be hyperactive, and are calmer and more alert in class. They also have an increased capacity to learn and are less likely to be absent from school.

See website www.foodforlifeuk.org

Eating a healthy balanced diet not only helps children to work better in schools. It serves to provide the building blocks for future health as well as increasing self-esteem and emotional wellbeing, as noted in Spotlight (ibid):

> Children and young people who fail to eat a balanced diet and meet recommended levels of physical activity face a disproportionately high risk of developing a range of life threatening conditions, including diabetes, heart disease and circulatory disorders…can also affect children and young people's quality of life and their emotional well-being…cause low self-esteem and depression as well as contributing to a range of behavioural problems.

Suggested letter to parents and carers

Whole-school involvement

Dear Parents and Carers,

Healthy eating programme

This term we are starting a healthy eating programme throughout the school as part of our work on PSHE (Personal, Social and Health Education) and 'healthy schools standard'. The children will be learning about how food is produced and how it is prepared or cooked for eating. Children will be growing foods, preparing foods and tasting them.

We would like your cooperation in this work and hope that you can help us to encourage the children to taste and eat a wider variety of foods.

We hope you can attend a whole-school meeting so that we can share our ideas for promoting healthy eating with you. As a school we can only do so much and very much need your help if we are to be successful in this programme.

The meeting will be on… (day) at… (time) in… (place) and we look forward to meeting you there.

Yours sincerely,

Suggested letter to parents and carers

For one class

Dear Parents and Carers

Healthy eating programme

This term we are starting a healthy eating programme in our class as part of our work in PSHE (personal, social and health education). The children will be learning about how food is produced and how it is prepared or cooked for eating. Children will be growing foods, preparing foods and tasting them.

We would like to tell you about this work and there will be a meeting after school in our classroom on… (date) so that we can talk about how we will present this work to the children. We welcome your cooperation and will discuss how together we can help children to feel good about the healthy eating programme as well as what you can do to help at home.

Yours sincerely,

Food Provided in School

The Department of Health has been working for some time (with input from National Confederation of Parent Teacher Associations (NCPTA)) to produce a new Food in Schools Toolkit. This contains ideas on a range of issues from growing clubs to lunchboxes. See the website www.foodinschools.org

It also states that:

> All primary school children must be given the opportunity to learn some basic practical cooking skills but to what extent is up to the individual school. In 1999 the Qualifications and Curriculum Authority (QCA) designed schemes of work for schools which relate to each curriculum subject and each year group. Schools are under no compulsion to follow these schemes but many schools do.

The school fruit and vegetable scheme

This was introduced after the NHS Plan 2000 included a commitment to implement a national school fruit scheme by 2004.

> We want schools to promote the 5 A DAY message, encouraging all children to eat at least five portions of fruit and vegetables a day and, where appropriate, join the School Fruit and Vegetable Scheme. By the end of 2004, all 4-6 year olds in LEA maintained infant, primary and special schools will be eligible for a free piece of fruit or vegetable every school day.
> Page 15 *Healthy Living Blueprint for Schools* (ibid)
> (See fact sheet for more information.)

Fruit in schools

A few schools do now provide fruit for all older children to eat before the morning break. This can be expensive. Perhaps parents can help, either by providing a piece of fruit or by giving money towards its purchase. The eating of fruit together in the classroom can provide a valuable social setting, especially when a variety of cut fruit is put on a platter to be passed around and chosen by each child.

School meals

You will need to involve the school catering arrangements to support you in this healthy eating programme. Healthier eating may mean more expense. Perhaps less choice will enable you to provide healthier options; you may need to start in a small way by introducing balanced alternatives and omitting less healthy foods. Discussion with your school caterers will be most important in making these decisions.

School lunches are a key area for improvement as they reinforce healthy eating messages from the classroom…can encourage pupils to eat more fruit and vegetables and develop a taste for food low in salt, sugar and fat. *Healthy Living Blueprint for Schools*, page 16.

The school day is very long for many children, especially those who do not have an adequate breakfast. Several schools have breakfast clubs and others are starting to provide breakfasts. Other schools encourage children to bring a healthy snack for break times.

Children need energy to get through the school day and break time snacks can provide some of that energy. A policy on food consumed at break time (or only selling healthy food) can help cut the levels of fat, sugar and salt that children consume and boost their intake of fruit and vegetables. *Healthy Living Blueprint for Schools*, page 16.

Few primary schools have tuck shops; if you have one you will need to look at what it sells, substituting healthier options for crisps, sweets and some drinks.

Drinks

The *Healthy Living Blueprint for Schools* states that:

All pupils should have access to drinking water at all times at a number of points around the school, preferably not from taps in the toilets. Pupils should be permitted to carry water with them and consumption encouraged both in class and during break and lunch-time. (Page 17)

More schools are encouraging children to bring bottles of water to school so that they can drink at will. Water is provided at lunch-time and children should be actively encouraged to drink this. Perhaps you can convince parents of children who bring packed lunches to send only water to drink instead of fizzy drinks or squash.

Packed lunches

Many parents opt for their children to take a packed lunch to school. The Food Standards Agency (FSA) has found that packed lunches may contain high levels of salt, fat and sugar. Schools can seek to influence the content of packed lunches and make advice to parents available. It is important to engage with parents and carers about the benefits and practicalities of providing a healthier packed lunch. *Healthy Living Blueprint for Schools*, page 17.

If you actively encourage parents to share this work that the children are doing you will be well on the way to helping them to realise their vital part in providing healthy balanced school lunchboxes.

So what is this book trying to do?

It is an attempt to bring balanced eating into the primary classroom and to give teachers ideas for promoting, growing and cooking foods so that children will enjoy preparing and tasting foods that might otherwise be unavailable to them. There are activities for children to learn about meals, ways to cook foods in the classroom, ways to grow vegetables as well as activities about the health benefits of drinking water.

The activities will easily slot into your PSHE programme as they all ask children to work co-operatively and socially in their search for more understanding of the things we eat and drink. The activities are meant to be fun.

Start in Circle Time

You can plan these activities with the children through Circle Time and carry them out later that day. You will need careful organisation of time and manpower in the classroom and will need to think of the best system for you to carry out activities. Your classroom assistant will be needed and teachers of young children may like to ask for volunteer parent help.

What You Get in This Book

While not really being about nutrition as such, this book is about encouraging children to focus on various foods and drinks so that they can make healthy choices. The aim of the activities is to help children aged five to nine to enjoy learning about foods and drinks in a fun way. It contains:

Letters for parents and carers

On pages 8 and 9 there are two suggested letters you may like to use to inform parents of the programme. At the front of each section there is a suggested letter to inform parents of what you are doing, seek their cooperation and ask them to tell you of any specific dietary needs of their child.

The way in

This page is to help to set the scene in Circle Time and give children an idea of what is to follow.

Draw and talk

These activities are for younger children.

Draw and write

These activities are for older children who are mainly able to write for themselves, although some may need the help of a scribe who will write what the child dictates.

Activities

You choose from the suggested activities those that are suitable for your children. Some have two strands; some are more suitable for younger or older children. You will know the abilities and interests of your children and can mix, match or amend the activities to suit them.

Each section has suggested one or more 'let's make it' activities that can dovetail into the section as presented or they can be used separately. You will need to organise these according to the age of your children, the help you have available and the situation of your setting. If at all possible it is preferred that the cooking aromas should permeate the classroom, so that all children can enjoy the smell of the cooking. Failing this you may have a school kitchen that will allow for children's foods to be cooked there. You may like to have an occasional whole morning or afternoon cooking activity, with all the children engaged in the activity or you may prefer each group to do the cooking on a different day during the same week. It is important to make sure that children wash their hands before cooking; this instruction precedes each making activity.

Food hygienists say that washing hands takes time – the time it takes to sing Happy Birthday all the way through once. Try it with the children and let them see you wash your hands. You will need a kitchen cleaning spray to make sure that the work surfaces are really clean before preparing any food.

Warning: make sure that children do not eat foods harmful to them. You will know if there is a child with an allergy in your class and will make sure that they do not taste foods that could be harmful to them.

Each section has a 'Let's grow it' activity. You may like to set this up before doing the main activities so that the food is already growing and can be a part of the work. Some schools have a school garden where you can plant seeds and watch them grow outdoors. You may prefer to use pots in the classroom so that children can care for them indoors and take them home to care for during school holidays. I recently visited a primary school in Hampshire where there was a very productive vegetable garden. All the foods had been grown by children in the school, from Year R to Year 6.

(The website http://www.teachernet.gov.uk/growingschools/ states its main focus is on reconnecting children with food production, farming and the countryside.)

At the end of each section there is a 'Let's reflect and share' activity, where children are encouraged to reflect on their work and take home something to share with their families

There are fact sheets with information for teachers in the appendix. You may like to duplicate some of these to send home. Each fact sheet is an abridged or simplified version of information obtained from websites which are listed; you can find out more by visiting the website. There is also a list of appropriate website addresses and books. The information from these may be appropriate for several sections.

It is hoped that you will adapt these cooking and growing ideas and be inspired to make or grow other healthy foods that the children can then share and eat.

The seven sections are:

breakfast
mid-day dinner
tea
supper/evening meal
barbecue
picnic
party or celebration meals.

What is healthy?

'Healthy' is a difficult word for children to understand so the introductory activity is about developing this understanding by asking the children to draw and talk or write about being healthy. It is important to use this word rather than 'well' or 'strong' because people who are not well can still be healthy, just as can those who are not strong. Those who have not used Draw and Talk or Write before will need to read the instructions in this introduction before starting this first and vital activity.

Those of you who have already used Circle Time, Draw and Talk and Draw and Write can skip the following pages!

Circle Time Framework

The framework involves very small circles or even groups for the youngest children and a regular pattern, with:

- welcome – a name using activity – (for example, 'Good morning, Tasha'.)

- teacher's time – for informal exchange of information.

- children's time, for telling important views.

- the 'meat' of the session – in this case one of the sections.

- a fun ending – for example, a game or a song.

- explicit rules so that children know exactly what is expected of them.

Involving techniques

In Circle Time it is really important to involve all the children and so the first activity and some others have various techniques to help children to feel involved. They are:

- wave – wave a hand if you agree

- raise a hand/thumb or put a hand on shoulders to show that you agree or are involved in the idea

- pass the sentence – repeat the sentence with your own ending to the next person and pass it around the circle

- question and answer – answer the question from one person, turn and ask the question to the next person

- change places – when the same word/response is given by different children ask them to change places with the child who most recently gave that response

- pass the face – show by facial expression what you think and pass this face around the circle. When used to this technique, older children can move their expression around the circle very quickly.

- stand and show – children bring their work to the circle and, when asked, stand and show their picture to the whole group. With small groups you may like the children to walk around the inside of the circle, showing their picture. Children who, for some personal reason, may not want to show their work should not be asked to do so

- vote with your feet – if children are to vote on some aspect of the work, select a specific area of the classroom and ask children to move there, for example, stand near the window if you think… Then ask the children to count themselves.

Draw and Talk and Draw and Write

The activities in this book rely heavily on a technique called 'Draw and Talk' for younger children and 'Draw and Write' for older children. Draw and Talk is a simple drawing and talking activity, loosely based on the illuminative Draw and Write research strategies originally devised by Noreen Wetton, and now widely used in developing and evaluating curriculum programmes in health education.

Draw and Talk

During Circle Time ask the younger children to focus on some aspect of the topic, make a picture inside their heads about it and remember it so that they can draw it later. After the Circle Time session ask the children to draw that picture and as they finish their drawings give an individual opportunity for each child to talk to you about their drawing. Write down keywords (on their picture) from what they say and from what they tell you in response to the 'prompt' questions.

Draw and Write

This is used here as an opening activity for older children. It is similar to Draw and Talk and can be a whole class activity. Give older children specific instructions to draw; ask them not to share their drawing with others. The drawing activity helps to concentrate them on the topic; once they are all drawing, stop them and ask them to write about their drawing in response to specific instructions. As they finish their writing, encourage them to finish their drawings.

Make a display

Mount these pictures (with the keywords you have written from Draw and Talk and children's writing from Draw and Write). Add captions/questions drawn from the children's responses to make a display. Share this initial work with families, other teachers, governors and use it as a starting point (baseline data) in the children's learning. As you progress through the activities add more work to the display, which will grow and give you a picture of the children's learning. At the end of the section, revise and remember all the good work and positive messages from the children.

Children can evaluate and celebrate their work

Following your teaching, intervention, activities and discussions, you can repeat the Draw and Talk activity to find out changes in each child's perceptions. You could add the second set of children's pictures to the display or include both sets of drawings in the children's individual records. Discuss with the children their changed perceptions and increased knowledge and let them see how much they have learned. Help the children to celebrate how much they have learned.

How to organise Draw and Talk

The way you organise this will depend on the circumstances of your setting, the way you plan your day and the number of adults who can supervise the children while one adult asks each child to talk.

In nursery, preschools or Year R

With a good ratio of adults to children it is possible to do this as a small group activity while other children are engaged in various activities. Before ending the pre-activity Circle Time discussion, explain that small groups of two, four or six children will be sitting with you so that they can do their drawings undisturbed. As each child completes their drawing take them to one side or to an adjoining table/chair and ask them about their drawing. Use the pre-determined questions as triggers to enable each child to have the same experience of talking about their picture. As each child tells you about their drawing, write key words about what they say in a corner of the child's paper. Conclude this part of the activity by asking them to help you to write a sentence about their picture. Ask the child if there is anything else they want to tell about their picture and when the answer is finally 'no', thank them for the picture and say you are going to put it in a safe place because it is important and special and you will want to look at it again. Very young children, used to taking their work home to share with parents or carers, may be reluctant to relinquish their picture, but you can point out that you want to keep it because it is so very special and important.

In Key Stage 1 classes

These children will use the Draw and Write activity. There is usually a classroom helper available to help. They (or a volunteer parent) can 'scribe' for children who are just starting to write for themselves. Scribes must write only what the child asks them to write and resist the temptation to help with suggestions of what they think the children may want to say. These older infants can do the drawing and writing as a whole-class activity. Encourage them to use their own spellings.

In Key Stage 2 classes

Key Stage 2 children will have little difficulty in writing about their pictures. It is important to make sure that they do their own work without sharing or discussing it with other children. The whole-class discussion after the work is the most important part of the activity.

Children who have very special needs

The activities in this book lend themselves to those who work with children with special needs – either in special schools or in mainstream schools where children work in small groups with a helper. Older children can use the Draw and Write/Talk to good effect and although they may need help with some of the activities, the discussions – on a one to one basis with a helper – will give them a platform for their ideas, increasing their confidence and self-worth.

As a whole–school activity

If you are going to do the Draw and Talk/Write as a whole-school activity, perhaps to compare some of the children's responses in order to evaluate your work, you will need to make sure that the activity is undertaken in exactly the same way with each class using exactly the same content and trigger questions. Any deviation will make cross year comparison impossible. Scribes must write only what the child asks them to write – resisting the temptation to help with suggestions of what they think the children may want to say.

Use only the suggested reminders to keep the children on track – if you deviate you will not be able to compare responses with other classes or previous/following years.

How will you use Draw and Talk or Draw and Write?

Use it:

- as a tool to set the scene for Circle Time discussion
- as a starting point to consider various aspects of children's contributions
- to share the children's common perceptions about the section/topic
- as a means of ensuring that you listen individually to each child at some time
- to make a display of the children's pictures to give 'voice' to their work
- as a 'before and after' to check the success of your teaching programme
- to evaluate some common section throughout the year/school
- as a celebration of all that the children know and can tell you.

Introductory Activities

The whole idea of 'health' and 'being healthy' is difficult for young children to understand. Many will equate it to being well or whole, to being not ill or to being strong. We need help children to try to understand what the words 'health' and 'a healthy lifestyle' mean and that there are many healthy lifestyles for different people.

One approach is to ask the children to draw a healthy person and to draw the things they need to help to live a healthy lifestyle. Talking together about what they have drawn will help children to begin to understand the concept of health. Healthy eating is only one part of a healthy lifestyle and in this introduction we can help children to understand that other factors such as exercise, rest, cleanliness as well as loving and being loved (mental health) all play a part in living a healthy lifestyle.

There are many healthy lifestyles – what suits you may not be right for me; this activity is a starter to open the children's eyes to all the possibilities of living a healthy lifestyle before concentrating on healthy eating.

The introductory activity 'a healthy person' will open up this subject for debate which can be followed by the Circe Time discussion.

A healthy person Draw and Talk for younger children

Tell the children that you think they all look really healthy today. Say that you would like them all to draw a picture of a person who looks really healthy.

After a few minutes add, 'Draw what your person is doing that helps them to be healthy.'

As the children finish their pictures ask them to come to you (or the classroom helper) in a quiet place to talk about their picture. As each child tells you about their picture write keywords in a corner of the paper.

Ask each child these prompt questions:

- How can I tell from your picture that this is a healthy person?

- What are they doing in your picture to be healthy?

- What else could they do to keep healthy?

Come together as a group and share the children's work, first looking together at the pictures they have drawn. Are all the pictures smiling? Ask if this means they are healthy. Are they all doing healthy things? Make a list of these healthy things. Read through the list and see if the children have mentioned exercise, rest, cleanliness, eating and drinking and love (mental health).

Explain that all these things help us to be healthy. Have any drawn children wearing glasses? Are these people healthy? Have any drawn someone in a wheelchair? Is this person healthy? Can people who are ill or who have to take medicines be healthy?

Explain that being healthy is important to everyone, even if they seem to be ill or different from the rest of us. 'Healthy' is not to do with being strong or being well, it is to do with looking after our body, feeding it, exercising it, resting it and keeping it clean. It has also to do with loving and being loved – that keeps our feelings healthy.

Display the pictures under a title 'We look after our body to keep it healthy'. Write in speech bubbles the words eating, drinking, resting, exercising, cleaning and loving. Talk about the pictures often so that the children know what healthy is.

A healthy person Draw and Write for older children

Tell the children that you think they all look really healthy. Say that you want them all to draw a picture and do some writing about someone who is healthy.

Explain the rules for Draw and Write, to use their own ideas without sharing them and without talking about what they are drawing.

Remind them to be ready to stop drawing and start the writing when asked and:

- not to worry about spellings
- to ask the scribe in a whisper to write what they say if they need help
- to go back to finish their drawing when they have written all they can.

Ask them to fold their paper in half and to draw on one half, keeping the other for their writing. As the children are drawing ask them to stop drawing and to write about:

- how they know this person is healthy, how does the person look?
- what the person is doing in the picture that is helping them to keep healthy
- what else the person could do to keep healthy.

Give them time to finish their work. Ask the children to bring their work to the circle to talk about it together. Ask volunteers to say what they have written about the first instruction. Can others add to that? Make a list of what they say. Read through the list; does everyone agree? Have any of them drawn someone who is limping, has a broken arm, cannot walk or showing any other injury? Ask if these people can be healthy. Explain that people who are sick or have same disability can still be healthy.

Ask volunteers to say what they have written about the latter two instructions and make a second list. Read through this list – does everyone agree that these are the things that we do to keep healthy? Have they included exercise, rest, cleanliness, food and drink? Explain that all these things are needed if we are to keep our body healthy. Have any included love? Explain that this is needed if they are to have a healthy mind. You may like to make a display of this 'being healthy and keeping healthy' work for children from other classes to share.

Remind the children that eating, drinking, resting, exercising, keeping clean, loving and being loved are all important for a healthy body and a healthy mind.

Circle Time discussion

It is important to talk to children about different foods before you start this programme. A 'healthy diet' or 'healthy eating' are difficult phrases for young children to comprehend. Not only is 'healthy' difficult but the word 'diet' itself has connotations with slimming and eating special foods because there may be something wrong with you.

Explain that all foods have some goodness in them that satisfy hunger.

- Some foods are really good for us and help all the bits of our bodies to grow up really healthily.

- Some foods are 'OK' foods, they stop us being hungry and help us to grow, but they don't help our bodies to grow especially well.

- Some foods are not so good for us but we like them and can have them as treats.

Explain to the children that we need to keep a balance in the foods we eat and the liquids we drink. Too much of anything cannot be good for us. Make sure that the children realise that treats are really OK and that we all like treats, but that if we only ever eat 'treat' foods our bodies will not grow up to be healthy bodies and we can be unhealthy grown-ups as we get older.

Talk about the things that they like to eat and what foods come under which heading: really good body building foods, OK foods, only as treats.

Talk about the things that they like to drink and remind the children that fizzy drinks are OK for treats but that if they only ever drink fizzy drinks, and never drink water, their bodies may become unhealthy as they get older. Water is the best drink of all and as long as they are drinking some water each day their bodies will be able to cope with a few other kinds of drinks.

You may like to talk about people who are vegetarians and those who have allergies to certain foods, such as milk or peanuts. This helps to explain that there is not one 'healthy diet' for us all, but there are many different ways of balanced eating and as they grow older they will find the way that works for them. While they are young it is important to make sure that they get the basic building blocks so that they will grow up with healthy bodies.

Now we've got that out of the way, let's start learning about foods that we eat, how they are grown and how we prepare or cook them.

What better place to start than breakfasts!

Section 1: Breakfast

In this section the children will be thinking about what they eat at breakfast time and how some of these foods are prepared.

Let's taste it – orange drinks

You will need a pack of fresh orange juice, and a pack of not fresh juice, a pack of orange drink and orange squash, large jugs, cups.

Let's make it – porridge

You will need some porridge oats.

Let's grow it – oats

You will need some oat seeds or grass seed.

You will also need:

- empty food packaging as suggested in the homework section of 'The way in'

- a carton each of skimmed, semi-skimmed and full fat milk for the milk activity

- very small cups or measuring caps for tasting

- a jar of honey.

Suggested letter to parents and carers before starting work on this section

Dear Parents or Carers,

Breakfasts

As part of our work on balanced eating we will be learning about and doing activities about breakfasts. As you know, breakfast is a very important meal, especially for children. It is thought that children who have a nutritionally good breakfast are more ready and able to learn. Children who become hungry during the morning may not be good learners.

We will be looking at the kinds of food and drink that people have for breakfast and asking children to tell us about what they have to eat and drink. We will be learning about foods and drinks such as milk, fruit juice, cereals, honey and eggs. The children will be making porridge and growing oats or grasses as well as tasting different kinds of milk.

We hope that you will show your child that you are interested in this topic and support them in this learning. If your child has any special dietary needs please make sure we know about them before we start this work.

Yours sincerely

Breakfast

The way in...

In Circle Time start by talking about your breakfast. What did you have to eat this morning?

Ask the children to finish the sentence: 'For breakfast this morning I had...' Jot down on the board what the children say to make a list. When all the children have finished, read the list to them and talk about the different foods and drinks.

Ask volunteers to say what they would like to have for breakfast – perhaps the things they have at the weekend, or on special occasions. Make a list of these things and link any that are on the previous list.

Talk to the children about the importance of having a good breakfast, one that will last them until lunch time, one that will be good for their bodies and help them to grow up well and healthy.

Tell the children that you want to draw a green ring around the foods and drinks in both lists that they think are especially healthy. Ask volunteers to say which things ought to have a green ring around them. Ask those who agree to wave a hand.

> For breakfast this morning we had...
>
> corn flakes
> Coco Pops
> milk
> toast
> egg
> bread
> cereal
> porridge
> sausage
> bacon
> orange juice.

Explain that some foods have a lot of sugar, fats and salt in them and may not be quite so good at keeping them well and healthy. Explain that what is in food has to be listed on the packet. Tell the children that you want to draw a red ring around any of the foods in both lists that they think have a lot of sugar, salt or fat in them. Talk about all these foods and whether we should add more sugar, salt or fat to them.

Before ending the Circle Time session ask the children to close their eyes and think of the breakfast they had today. Ask them to make a picture in their heads of this breakfast and tell them that you will want them to draw this picture later.

Homework

Ask the children to bring in:

- packets or labels from breakfast cereals

- some empty egg boxes

- empty drinks cartons from drinks they have at breakfast time.

Younger Children

Draw and Talk

Ask the children to draw the picture of themselves having their breakfast. Ask them to draw all the foods that they like to eat and drink for breakfast. Ask them to colour in the foods that they think are really healthy, that will help their bodies to grow especially well.

As the children finish their pictures ask them to come to you (or the classroom helper) in a quiet place to talk about their picture.

As each child tells you about their picture write keywords of foods in a corner of the picture.

Ask each child these three prompt questions:

1. What do you like to eat for your breakfast?

2. What do you like to drink for your breakfast?

3. Which of these foods you have drawn do you think will be really good at helping your body to grow up to be really healthy?

Breakfast

Coco Pops
milk
toast
egg.

Milk and egg would be good for my body.

If I didn't have breakfast I would feel hungry. I would ask my mum for some.

Then ask each child what would happen if they didn't have any breakfast at all. How would they feel? What would they do?

Take the drawings to the next Circle Time and ask the children if you can show their pictures to everyone and read out the things they have said.

Talk about the most popular breakfasts. You could make a list of all the foods they have drawn. Talk about:

*   the most popular breakfast cereal

*   fruit or a fruit drink

*   which foods and drinks the children think are the healthiest

*   which may not be quite so healthy.

Talk about the foods that have only a little sugar, salt and fat in them and those that have a lot of these things. Make a display of all these pictures with the children's comments around them in large speech bubbles. Add your own questions. Ask the children to think of a title.

Older Children

Draw and Write

Explain the rules for Draw and Write, to use their own ideas without sharing them and without talking about what they are drawing. Remind them to be ready to stop drawing and start the writing when asked and:

- not to worry about spellings

- to ask the scribe in a whisper to write what they say if they need help

- to go back to finish their drawing when they have written all they can.

I am having Weetabix and milk and then I'll have some bread and jam and a drink of tea. I chose it because I like it. I feel full.

Ask the children to think about the picture they made in their heads in Circle Time. Then ask them to fold their paper in half and on one half to draw this picture of themselves having their breakfast. After the children have had a few minutes to draw, stop them and ask them to write on the other half of the paper about:

- what they are eating for their breakfast

- what they are drinking for their breakfast

- who chose their breakfast

- whether they liked that breakfast

- how they are feeling as they are eating and drinking their breakfast.

As the children are writing, walk around the class and remind them of the things you asked them to write about.

When all the children have finished their drawing and writing, ask them to come together as a group to talk about what they have drawn and written and their feelings about breakfast time. How many of the children have drawn fruit, fruit juice or yoghurt? How many drew a milky drink? Talk about which foods and drinks the children think are the healthiest and which are not so healthy. Explain that it is very important to have a good breakfast before they come to school.

Talking about and sharing what the children have drawn and written is a vital part of this work. You may like to use some of the pictures and writing to make a display.

Activities

Milk

see website http://schoolfs.wisdairy.com/ and www.milk.co.uk

NB Ensure that children who do not drink cow's milk or who have milk intolerance do not taste milk. You may like to pair these children with someone who does drink milk to work together on this activity.

Talk about dairy farms and how we get milk from cows. Talk about different kinds of dairy cows, how cows used to be milked and present day mechanisation. Talk about cleanliness and pasteurisation and integrate this work with topics such as 'farming' or 'the environment'. Perhaps you could visit a dairy farm.

To see the milking process from cow in the field through the milking parlour visit the website www.greenheyes.com/pages/milking01.htm You can either download and print the pictures to make up your own poster or show older children how to do this. You may like to ask children to work in pairs to download and print some of these pictures and text so that children can make their own book about dairy-farming. Ask them to add their own words to explain each picture. (There are other pages on this website with pictures of cows and other animals in fields.)

Bring into the classroom four cartons of milk – full fat, semi-skimmed, skimmed and soya. Duplicate the activity sheet 'Milk' from the end of this section or the CD and tell the children that you want them, in turn, to taste each type milk and write down their feelings about it. Set up a tasting counter, with small cups where children can taste the four kinds of milk.

Cereals and porridge

Before this session ask the children to bring in different kinds of empty cereal boxes or labelling.

Talk about cereals and porridge. Ask the children how many of them have cereal for breakfast. Ask them if they know where these foods come from and what they contain. Explain that these are based on grains which are sometimes processed and sometimes natural.

If you have a lot of labels and packets give a selection to each group and ask them to examine them and write out their contents as a group list. If you have only a few, put them on a table and ask each group in turn to visit the table and make a list of contents.

Come together as a class and talk about their findings. Note the number of cereals that have added sugar, salt, fat and make a list of these. Note the number that are completely natural and make a list of these.

Ask the children who add extra sugar to their cereal and make a note of this. Ask the children if they know that eating too much sugar is bad for teeth. Explain that sugar gives us energy and that this energy is immediate. Explain that the cereal itself also gives us energy but that this is slow energy that will last them until lunch-time.

Corn flakes

These already have sugar added.
14 children have these for breakfast and
10 put more sugar on them.

Eggs

Before the session, collect the empty egg boxes that the children bring to school so that you can talk about the different ways that eggs are marketed.

Ask the children how many of them have an egg for breakfast. If any do, ask them whether they have this boiled, fried, scrambled, poached or as an omelette. Talk about these different ways of cooking eggs.

Ask the children what they know about how we get our eggs. Do they know that they come from hens? Talk about the different ways of keeping hens to produce eggs – free-range, barn and battery. Explain to the children these different ways and talk about our responsibility towards animals and the conditions of hens in the various farms that produce eggs.

Talk about what the hens eat (free-range hens) – worms and grubs as well as chicken food. Talk about what food manufacturers also give to hens – pellets of food that contain nourishment but that may have additives in them. Explain that organic free-range eggs are the best but are very expensive.

Ask the children if they know how eggs are used in cooking. Do they know that they are used in making cakes, pancakes, meringues or pies?

Ask the children to draw themselves eating an egg that has been cooked in their favourite way. Ask them to write about where the egg came from, who cooked it, they way it was cooked and whether they liked it a lot or a little.

Read out some of the information from the fact sheet in the appendix. You may prefer to edit this for younger children.

English breakfast

Ask the children if they can tell you what a 'full English breakfast' is. List their responses, asking other

'Full English'

bacon   black pudding
mushrooms   tomatoes
eggs   sausage
baked beans
fried potato
fried bread.

children to add to these if they can. Have they offered you all the ingredients that go to make this meal? When you have a full list, ask the children to think whether having this kind of breakfast every day of the week is a good idea. Are there some foods that have too much fat to eat every day? Which are these?

Continental breakfast

Ask the children if any have had a continental breakfast while abroad on holiday. If so, ask volunteers to tell you what this breakfast has. If not, list the contents, croissants, butter, preserves, yoghurt, fruit, coffee or chocolate to drink. In some countries people eat hard-boiled eggs, slices of cheese or ham as well as toast. Ask the children to draw two plates, one with an English breakfast and the other with a continental one. Which do they think is the healthiest? Ask older children to write about the differences.

Other breakfasts

If you have children from various cultures in your class ask them to tell you what they have for their breakfast. Ask them to explain about any foods that are different from the English and Continental breakfasts. You may be able to persuade their parent or carer to bring in some of these foods to talk about and show to the rest of the class.

Honey

Ask the children if any of them have eaten honey. If they have, ask these children to tell the others what it is like and how they eat it. Ask them if they know where honey comes from. Explain that it comes from bees and that there are beekeepers all over the world that keep bees in hives just to collect honey. Bring in a jar of honey so that the children can see and taste it. You will need a supply of spoons – perhaps plastic ones or some from the school kitchen. Make sure that the children put only clean spoons into the honey and put dirty spoons into a bowl of water to be washed. When they have all tasted it, ask for a show of hands from those who like it. Ask the children to give you words about how it tastes.

Explain that honey tastes differently according to the flowers that the bees have visited. Tell them that in Spain you can buy orange or lemon blossom honey because the beekeepers know that their bees have only visited the large orange groves there.

It would be interesting if you have access to a honeycomb or know a local beekeeper who would come in to talk to the children about keeping bees. Explain that the honeycomb is in the shape of a hexagon. You could make some interesting patterns using honeycomb templates. You may like to talk about quilts that are made using these shapes.

Breakfast drinks

Ask the children to tell you what they like to drink at breakfast time. Ask them to finish the sentence: 'For breakfast I like to drink…' Collect their responses and make a list on the board. Which is the most popular drink? Which do the children think is the healthiest? How many children drink fruit juice?

Ask them to examine the empty drinks packets they brought in. For younger children read out the contents and talk about the juice and sugar content of them all. Which is the healthiest?

Ask older children to work in pairs to investigate the information and make a chart of this data. Ask them to generate a table of results by hand or on the computer, highlighting those with the most fruit content and the least added sugar.

Let's taste it – orange drinks

Set out a tasting counter using the four jugs of drinks: fresh orange, orange squash, long life orange and orange drink labelled 1, 2, 3, 4. Ask the children to taste each drink and to decide which they prefer. Collect the data on the board or make a chart. Then tell the children which drink each number represented. Examine the cartons and ingredients. Ask the children to decide which drink they think is the best.

Tell the children the cost of each drink and how long it would keep before going off. Talk about which is the best option, bearing in mind the keeping qualities of the drinks and the price. If you have a juicer you could juice and taste the whole fruit of oranges.

Which is best?

We tasted all the drinks. Most of us liked number 3 best. This was the fresh juice (15).

Lots of us liked number 1, the longlife drink best (12).

One of us liked number 2, the orange drink best.

None of us liked number 4 best. This was the squash.

We think the fresh juice is best for you but it costs the most. The longlife juice is a good option.

We think water is better for you than the squash.

Let's make it – porridge or muesli

Make sure that you and the children wash hands before this activity.

If you have access to a cooker, the children could make some porridge.

Explain that it is made from oats and that Scotland is a place that produces oats and that a lot of porridge comes from there. Tell them that most Scots put salt on their porridge, not sugar.

Explain that oats are a whole grain and that these are good and healthy foods. You may like to let one group at a time make porridge.

Put one small cupful of porridge into a pan (preferably non-stick) and add two cups full of cold water. Put the pan onto the heat and stir carefully until the porridge boils. Some porridge only needs to come to the boil and then stand for a few minutes, others need to simmer for a few minutes; there will be instructions on your packet. You could use a microwave.

Put a little into small bowls, one for each child and ask them to add a little honey or sugar and some milk to cool it. Ask how many of them like porridge.

You could do this activity with home made muesli instead of porridge. You'll need to gather the ingredients and allow the children to measure the amounts and mix them. Delia Smith's muesli ingredients are 225 grams each of wholewheat flakes, rye flakes, oat flakes, barley flakes, raisins, 350 grams unsalted roasted peanuts, 175 grams sunflower seeds, 450 grams sultanas. You can add dried banana and dried apricots too.

Let's grow it – oats

If you have access to a farm you may be able to collect a few ears of corn, barley, oats or wheat. Ask the children to sprinkle a very little on some damp soil and watch it grow. If you cannot get these grains, use grass seed, explaining that the grains we eat are special kinds of grass. Watch the grain grow until it flowers and then collect the seeds. Open the seeds and find the nourishment inside. Ask older children to record the process.

Let's reflect and share

Remind the children that they have been learning about breakfast foods. Can they now tell you what a healthy breakfast is? Do some of them help to make the breakfast at home? Do any of them make breakfast for themselves or their parents or carers on their special days?

Ask younger children to draw pictures of breakfasts to share this work with their families. Ask older children to write a fact sheet about healthy breakfast foods, to write the recipe for porridge and to share this learning with their families at home. Perhaps they could make porridge for someone at home. Ask them to write down how oats are grown. You may like them to take home the fact sheet about hens and eggs in the appendix.

Remind them that no food is bad for them, but that some foods are healthier for them than others and that some foods that are not quite so healthy can be used as treats.

Milk

My name is _____

Draw the carton of red top milk	Draw the carton of green top milk	Draw the carton of blue top milk	Draw the carton of soya milk
How did it taste?	How did it taste?	How did it taste?	How did it taste?
How did it make you feel when you tasted it?	How did it make you feel when you tasted it?	How did it make you feel when you tasted it?	How did it make you feel when you tasted it?

Which milk is the creamiest?

Which milk is the sweetest?

I liked the........................... milk best because.................….............................

....

....

Turn over the page. Draw a picture of yourself drinking the kind of milk you like. Write about your picture.

Section 2: Dinner

In this section the children will be thinking about what they eat for their main meal whether it is at mid-day or evening and how some of these foods are prepared. You will need packaging as suggested in the homework section of 'The way in'.

Let's make it – salad

You will need salad vegetables.

Let's make it – fruit salad

You will need fruits, orange juice and sharp knives.

Let's grow it – beans

You will need:

- bean seeds

- compost

- trays.

Suggested letter to parents and carers before starting work on this section

Dear Parents or Carers,

Dinner

As part of our work on balanced eating we will be learning about and doing activities about the main meal of the day, sometimes called lunch and sometimes called dinner. Some people eat this at 12 noon and others eat it during the evening.

We will be looking at the kinds of food and drink that people have for their main meal and asking children to tell us about what they like to have to eat and drink. We will be learning about foods such as milk products, salt, fats and vegetables. The children will be making salads and fruit salads and we hope to grow some beans.

As you know nutritionists are worried about the amount of salt that people are eating and we will be helping children to understand that we should only eat a small amount of salt. We will also be looking at the different kinds of fats and talking about the fats that are really good for us, which we call 'good fats' and those which we call 'not so good fats' that we should eat only as treats.

We hope that you will show your child that you are interested in this topic and support them in this learning. If your child has any special dietary needs please make sure we know about them before we start this work.

Yours sincerely

Dinner

The way in...

In Circle Time start by talking about dinner. Tell the children that some people have a large mid-day meal and call it dinner and that others have a small mid-day meal and call it lunch. Talk about what the children call their main meal of the day.

Explain that this section is all about the main meal of the day whether they have it at mid-day or in the evening. Ask the children to think about what we eat for this meal. Ask the children to finish the sentence: 'For dinner we have...' Jot down on the board what the children say to make a list. When all the children have finished, read the list to them and talk about the foods.

Ask the children to look at the list and think about what they think are the really healthy foods and which are the foods that are not quite so healthy. Tell the children that you want a green circle around the foods that will help their bodies to grow healthily. Which foods can have a green circle? Talk about foods that are natural and not processed and about foods that they can eat raw.

For dinner we have...

meat
potatoes
peas
burgers
fish
cauliflower
cabbage
gravy
sausages
pies
chips
chicken.

Draw a blue ring around all the vegetables and fruits. Can children add more? Ask children to 'pass the face' to show if they like or dislike each one.

Now ask the children to think about a dinner meal including a school dinner meal that they really like. Ask them to finish the sentence 'For dinner, I like to eat...' Make a list of these responses on the board. How many have mentioned vegetables? How many mentioned meats? How many mentioned puddings and fruit? Ask the children which of these are really healthy foods and can have a green ring around them. Which are not so healthy and should be just for treats?

Before ending the Circle Time session ask the children to close their eyes and think of a mid-day meal they would like to have. Ask them to make a picture in their heads of the two plates of food and tell them that you will want them to draw this picture later.

Homework

Ask the children to bring washed packaging/labels from processed foods such as pizza, fish fingers, chicken bites, pies, puddings and ice cream.

Younger Children

Draw and Talk

Ask the children to think of themselves having the main meal they like best. Ask them to draw two plates, one for the main course and one for a sweet or pudding.

As the children finish their pictures ask them to come to you (or the classroom helper) in a quiet place to talk about their picture.

As each child tells you about their picture write keywords of foods in a corner of the picture.

Ask each child these three prompt questions:

1.   What else do you like to eat for your dinner?

2.   What do you like to drink at dinner time?

3.   Which of these foods you have drawn do you think will be really good at helping you to grow up well and healthy?

Dinner

meat
potatoes
beans
apple pie
ice cream
fizzy drink.

Meat and potatoes are healthy.

Take the drawings to the next Circle Time and ask the children if you can show their pictures to everyone and read out the things they have said.

Talk about the most popular foods and drinks. Make a chart of these and put alongside it the food information about the contents of these cereals. You could write a label explaining why some may be more healthy foods and drinks.

Talk about foods that have been specially cooked the day they are eaten from fresh ingredients. Talk about foods that have been processed using unknown ingredients then frozen and warmed up. Which do the children think could be better for us?

Explain the difference between fresh foods and processed and that sometimes these processed foods can be OK but that sometimes they have things that are not quite so good for our bodies. Ask the children to say what they think these not so healthy things could be. For example, colourings, preservatives, salt, sugar and extra fat.

Older Children

Draw and Write

Explain the rules for Draw and Write, to use their own ideas without sharing them and without talking about what they are drawing. Remind them to be ready to stop drawing and start the writing when asked and:

- not to worry about spellings

- to ask the scribe in a whisper to write what they say if they need help

- to go back to finish their drawing when they have written all they can.

Ask the children to think about the picture they made in their heads in Circle Time. Then ask them to fold their paper in half and on the top half to draw this picture of two plates – a first course and a sweet or pudding – and a drink. After the children

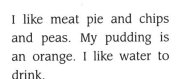

I like meat pie and chips and peas. My pudding is an orange. I like water to drink.

I feel happy with my dinner and pudding.

have had a few minutes to draw, stop them and ask them to write on the other half of the paper about:

- what is on their dinner plate

- what is on their other plate

- what they are drinking.

- how they are feeling as they are eating and drinking.

When all the children have finished their drawing and writing, ask them to join you in a group or circle to talk about what they have drawn and written and their feelings about their mid-day dinner.

How do the children feel about vegetables and fruit? How do they feel about chips? Which of the foods they have drawn do the children think are the healthiest? Which are not so healthy? Make a note of these responses to use in a display of the children's drawings and writing.

Talking about and sharing what the children have drawn and written is a vital part of this work.

Activities

Healthy dinner time foods

Remind the children about their drawings and what they said about them. Can they give you a list of the healthiest foods?

Make a list of all these foods and talk about why the children think these are healthy. Have they included vegetables and fruit? Have they included any processed foods?

Five a day

Help the children to learn these jingles about healthy eating:

Five a day, five a day	Lettuce, tomato, cucumber, eat quite a few
Let's eat five a day	These are the things that are good for you
Vegetables, fruits	Cabbages and carrots eat quite a bit
Leaves, stems and roots.	These will make you healthy and fit.
Eat to grow healthy	Bread or grains, eat every meal
Eat to grow well	These will help you all to feel
Eat for your body	Healthy and happy all the day
To be sound as a bell.	Eat them, eat them, don't say nay!
Five a day, five a day	Crisps and chocolate, hardly any
Let's eat five a day	These are treats so don't eat many.
Vegetables, fruits	Cakes and biscuits, also sweets
Leaves, stems and roots.	Just remember these are treats!

Ask the children to make up rhymes, jingles, songs or poems about eating five fruits and vegetables a day. They can use them as skipping rhymes.

Ready made foods

Collect the labelling from the food packaging that the children have brought in. Ask the children to help you to separate them in to main course and second course foods. Explain that food labelling has to show the amounts of sugar, fat and salt in each, and that these figures can be totals or per 100 grams.

With younger children read out the labels and talk about what is in each of the foods. Explain that foods that are packaged in factories need to have additives and preservatives in them to stop them from going bad. Ask these younger children to pick out and draw the foods they would like to have at dinner time for main course and second course. Talk about their pictures and which of these foods they think will be the best for their bodies.

Give groups of older children a collection of packages and ask different groups to investigate main course and sweet course foods. If there are not sufficient, make this a group activity with each group visiting a 'label table' during the day to carry out the investigation.

Ask them to work as a group to investigate each of the labels and collect data. Tell them that you want one final chart listing of the contents per 100 grams of each food. Come together as a class to talk about the contents of the various foods. If the groups are working on different labels ask a small group or pair of children to make two final lists with all the main course foods and all the second course foods. They could use the computer to generate a print-out for you to display.

Examine the findings and talk about whether the meals are healthy in terms of added fats, sugar and salt. Do the main course meals or sweet course meals seem the healthiest for us?

Milk products

Ask the children if they know the things that are made from milk. Make a list of the ones they know. Add to their list so that it is complete. Explain that milk contains fat that we call 'animal fat', because it comes from an animal.

Can the children tell you some of the things we need milk to make, such as custard, cakes, scones, cheese sauce and pancakes.

Ask the children to draw a picture of themselves eating their favourite food that needs milk. Ask older children to write about this food and to say why they like it.

> **Milk products**
>
> curds and whey
> cheese
> buttermilk
> butter
> yoghurt
> cream
> sour cream.

Salt

Ask the children whether they have salt on the table at school and home when they eat their main meal and make a note of this number. Ask how many of them shake salt onto their food and make a note of this number.

Ask the children to look at information about salt on the labels of the processed foods. To work out the amount of salt that's in a food, you have to work out how much you have eaten of the food. For example, if the label states the amount of sodium that's in 100g, you have to first multiply the amount by

2.5 to learn the amount of salt that's in there. This must then be multiplied by however much has been eaten to find the salt amount. The website www.salt.gov.uk explains further. Ask the children whether eating any of the foods would mean that they were eating more salt than they should.

What can they do to make sure they don't eat too much salt with their food? Ask how many children choose to shake salt onto their food. Has the number changed since the first time you asked them?

Fats

Explain to the children that we all need to eat some fat because it helps us to be healthy and to grow well. It is important to eat the right kinds of fat and not too much of it. Explain that feeding good fats to the body is also good for the brain. Fats in oily fish such as salmon, tuna, mackerel and sardines contain something called DHA (Docosahexsenoic Acid) which is good for the brain. Vegetable oils are good too. Animal fats are not quite so good.

On the board write the words monounsaturated fats, polyunsaturated fats and saturated fats and explain that these are the three kinds of fats that they will see on some food packaging.

Good fats		Not so good fats
Monounsaturated fats	Polyunsaturated fat	Saturated fats
canola oil olive oil.	safflower oil sunflower oil corn oil soybean oil.	all animal fats butter fat palm and palm kernel oil coconut oil cocoa butter (chocolate) hydrogenated oil partially hydrogenated oil.

Tell the children that some people like to eat fat on their meat but that many choose to cut the fat off their meat and not eat it. Ask whether they think there is any fat left in meat if you cut it all off. Make a note of the number who say 'no'. Explain that even in lean meats there is some animal fat.

Ask the children to look at the fat content on some of the food packaging. Most will list several kinds of fats in the same product. Ask older children to make two lists– one that contains the foods with good fats as well as the not so good fats and one that contains only foods with the not so good fats. Can they find any foods that list only the good fats?

Vegetables

Tell the children that the government says that healthy eating means we should eat at least five vegetables or fruits each day. Ask the children to think of all the vegetables that they know. Make a list on the board of all the vegetables that the children mention. Ask if any know others and if there are gaps, tell them about other vegetables and add them to the list. Read through the list with the children and ask each one to name their one favourite, writing a '1' alongside the name on the list until everyone has had a turn. Add up the marks to find the class favourite.

Ask younger children to think which of these vegetables they like cooked and which uncooked and ask them to draw and label these.

Ask older children to write two lists of all the vegetables they like; list one, with all the ones they like cooked and list two with the ones they like uncooked. Explain that there are things called vitamins in vegetables and that if vegetables are cooked for too long these vitamins get lost in the water. Some people keep the vegetable water to put in home made soups or casseroles. Some people used to add too much salt when cooking vegetables but we now know that this can spoil their flavour and is not good for us.

If possible enlist the help of a greengrocer, market stallholder or supermarket. Take each child, with a clipboard and paper, in small groups to this place and show them all the vegetables there and tell them the names. Ask them to draw some of the vegetables and write their names underneath, copying from the labels. Take back to school a small selection of the vegetables to examine; if in season include peas in the pod. Explain which of these vegetables are grown in this country and where the others are grown. Talk about the ones that need cooking and those that we eat raw. Show the children how to pod peas and eat a few raw.

www.thinkvegetables.co.uk invites you to download images of vegetables.

Tell the children that you want to find out who likes which vegetables, cooked and uncooked, and that you want to make charts so that you can show this.

Make two large charts, one for cooked vegetables and one for uncooked vegetables, with pictures of the vegetables along the top. Cut small identical rectangles of paper and explain that you want them to write their name on these papers so that they can paste them into the columns on the charts. Ask the children to suggest titles for the charts and display them in the classroom.

We like these cooked

Fun vegetables

Look at the fun vegetable poster and talk about what these vegetables might be. Do they all look happy? Do some look a bit scary? Why might they be scared? Will they like to be eaten? Older children might like to hear you read the poem *Vegetarians* by Roger McGough.

Give each child a copy of the poster and ask them to choose one vegetable that they like and to colour it in. Ask them to turn over the page and draw their own picture of this vegetable. Ask them to describe their chosen vegetable and to write a description of it in a speech bubble.

Can they write about how this vegetable is grown and how it is harvested? Do we eat it raw or do we cook it?

Ask older children to write a story about a vegetable character and to illustrate their story.

Let's make it – salad

Make sure that you and the children wash hands before this activity.

Select all the vegetables and fruits that we can use in salads and show the children how to clean them. Show the children how to cut them up using a sharp knife and board. With clean hands, ask volunteers to help to do this (a five year old is quite capable of using a sharp knife carefully when shown).

Ask the children to help to present the salad on a large dish. Give each child a paper napkin and either pass the dish around the circle so that children can take what they wish to eat, or put it on a table so that children can help themselves. Encourage children to try vegetables they may not have met before.

Let's make it – fruit salad

Make sure that you and the children wash hands before this activity.

Bring in, or ask the children to bring in, as many different kinds of fruit as you can. Talk about each fruit, how it is grown, where it is grown and how we prepare it for eating. Choose a selection that would be good in a fruit salad and let the children help with the peeling and cutting up of the fruits.

You may be able to make several large dishes – putting fruits of the same kind or colour together. Add orange juice to help the juices run together. Do not add sugar.

Ask the school kitchen to lend small bowls for children to make a choice of fruits to taste, otherwise use a clean spoon, and a bowl for washing them, if the children taste from the large bowls.

Let's grow it – beans

Runner beans are probably the quickest and easiest vegetable to grow. You may like to plant one or two in a jam jar lined with blotting paper. Sandwich the beans between glass and paper so that the children can see the root and stem growth. Add a little water which will be absorbed by the blotting paper.

Ask the children to bring in yoghurt pots. Using soil or potting compost show the children how to plant the beans and put them on a sunny windowsill to grow. Plant a few extras as spares. Watch and record their growth. You can use the activity sheet 'Growing beans'.

When they are large enough, the children who wish to can take theirs home to plant out in their garden. Others can be transplanted into large pots outside the classroom.

When they fruit, wash and eat some raw; cook others for the children to taste. (NB Some beans can be poisonous if eaten raw but I like to eat runner beans raw in salads.)

Let's reflect and share

Remind the children that they have been learning about foods we eat at mid-day lunch or dinner. Remind them of the 'five fruits or vegetables' rule for healthy eating. How many of them eat these every day?

Ask younger children to draw vegetables and fruits with the message 'Eat five a day'. Ask older children to write a fact sheet about fruit and vegetables to take home to their families with the 'five a day' message.

Do any of them help to cook at home? Ask them to make a fruit salad at home for their family. Afterwards ask them to talk about what they did and how their family liked it.

Remind them that no food is bad for them, but that some foods are healthier for them than others and that foods that are not quite so healthy can be used as treats.

Eat 5 a day

Growing Beans

My name is _____

Draw the pictures, write the dates and add some writing if you can.

The beans look like this:	We planted them in pots on.............. They look like this:
They look like this after one week:	They look like this after two weeks:
They look like this after three weeks:	The flowers look like this:
The beans are ....tall on.............:	The bean pods look like this: on ....:

Turn over the page and draw a picture of you eating a meal with beans. Write what kind of beans you are eating.

Section 3: Teatime

In this section the children will be thinking about teatime and what people eat for that meal.

You will need pictures and recipes of teatime foods as suggested in the homework section of 'The way in'.

You will need some jam jar labels.

Let's make it – biscuits

You will need flour, sugar and fat – butter or margarine.

Let's make it – bread

You will need strong flour, a little fat or olive oil, salt and a packet of dried yeast.

Let's grow it – cress

You'll need:

- a packet of cress

- some potting compound

- seed trays or food packaging trays.

Suggested letter to parents and carers before starting work on this section

Dear Parents and Carers

Tea

As part of our work on balanced eating we will be learning about and doing activities about teatime foods.

We will be looking at the kinds of food and drink that people have at teatime, even cream teas; asking children to say what they like to have to eat and drink. We will be learning about foods and drinks such as tea, different kinds of breads, cream, sugar and preserves.

The children will be tasting different kinds of breads and you may like to help us by trying out different kinds of breads at home with your family. We hope to make some bread to taste. We will also be making biscuits and talking about these as 'treat' foods rather than part of their everyday eating.

We hope that you will show your child that you are interested in this work and support them in this learning. If your child has any special dietary needs please make sure we know about them before we start this work.

Yours sincerely

Tea

The way in...

In Circle Time start by talking about afternoon tea. Tell the children that most people have a cup of tea and perhaps a biscuit in the middle of the afternoon but that some people have afternoon tea with sandwiches, cakes and pastries.

Cafés and restaurants sometimes serve cream teas where people drink tea and eat scones with cream. Talk about foods we eat as treats, not everyday foods; foods we like to eat sometimes which may contain a lot of sugar, salt or fat.

Ask the children to touch their nose if they have tea in the afternoon at their house, perhaps as soon as they get home from school. Ask volunteers to tell you what they have to eat and drink. Do they have tea to drink or do they have cold drinks?

Ask the children to finish the sentence 'For tea I would like...to eat.'

Ask them to finish the sentence, 'For tea I like... to drink.'

For tea I would like...

biscuits
cakes
buns
scones
lemon cake
sandwiches

squash, fruit juice, lemon, tea, coke, lemonade.

After each response ask those who also like it to touch their nose.

Did any children mention water to drink? Talk about water as a healthy drink.

Ask the children if they go out to visit their relations for tea sometimes. Ask volunteers to say whom they visit and what they have to eat and drink when they go to other people's houses for tea. Ask the children to think of going out to tea to a café or restaurant. What kinds of things do they like to eat and drink there?

Before ending the Circle Time session ask the children to close their eyes and think of what they most like to eat and drink at teatime. Ask them to make a picture in their heads of themselves having tea with their family and tell them that you will want them to draw this picture later.

Homework

Ask the children to look through old magazines at home and to cut out and bring pictures of foods, including recipes that people eat at teatime. Ask them to bring in washed cream cartons of any kind and labels from jam jars.

Younger Children

Draw and Talk

Ask the children to draw the picture of themselves having tea with their family. Ask them to draw all the food and drink that they would like to have for afternoon tea. Ask them to write the names of all the people in their picture.

As the children finish their pictures ask them to come to you (or the classroom helper) in a quiet place to talk about their picture.

As each child tells you about their picture write keywords of foods in a corner of the picture.

Ask each child these four prompt questions:

1. What else do you like to eat for tea?

2. What do you like to drink at teatime?

3. Which of these foods you have drawn do you think will be really good at helping you to grow up well and healthy?

4. Which of these foods are treats?

Afternoon tea

chocolate cake
biscuits
water or milk to drink.

Water is very healthy and chocolate cake is a treat.

Take the drawings to the next Circle Time and ask the children if you can show their pictures to everyone and read out the things they have said.

Ask the children to tell you:

- which is the most popular food

- which is the healthiest food

- which is the most popular drink

- which is the healthiest drink.

Ask the children to tell you:

- which of these foods are home made for them by a grown-up.

- which are bought from a shop ready made.

- which foods will help their body to stay healthy.

- which foods are treats – and why.

Older Children

Draw and Write

Explain the rules for Draw and Write, to use their own ideas without sharing them and without talking about what they are drawing. Remind them to be ready to stop drawing and start the writing when asked and:

- not to worry about spellings

- to ask the scribe in a whisper to write what they say if they need help

- to go back to finish their drawing when they have written all they can.

Ask the children to think about the picture they made in their heads in Circle Time. Then ask them to fold their paper in half and on the top half to draw their family having afternoon tea.

I drew cookies and bread and jam and a cup of tea. Wholemeal bread is healthy. Home-made cookies are healthy treats. They make me feel good.

After the children have had a few minutes to draw, stop them and ask them to write on the other half of the paper about:

- the food they have drawn

- the drink they have drawn

- which of these foods and drinks are really healthy and which are treats

- how they are feeling as they are eating and drinking.

When all the children have finished their drawing and writing, ask them to join you in a group or circle to talk about what they have drawn and written and their feelings about afternoon tea. Ask each child to 'stand and show' and to read out what they have written.

Make a list on the board of the foods and drinks that most children have drawn.

When all the children have finished reading, look at the list and ask the children to tell you which can have a green circle drawn around them to show that these are healthy foods and drinks. Talk about any foods and drinks that are not so healthy, that we like to have as occasional treats.

Talking about and sharing what the children have drawn and written is a vital part of this work.

Activities

Pictures and recipes

You may need to provide some teatime recipe pictures from magazines especially those from supermarket magazines. Collect the pictures and recipes that the children have brought in and ask the children to help you to sort them into things to eat and things to drink. Can they separate these into really healthy foods or treats?

Collect the recipes and look at the ingredients. Help the children to learn the ingredients of some of the foods such as cake and bread. Choose one of them and talk through the process of making that food. Explain any terms the recipe uses, such as 'rubbing in', 'beating' and 'folding'. Tell the children that you will be making some teatime biscuits soon and ask them what ingredients they think would be in biscuits.

Ask the children to draw one of the foods and to write down the things you would need to make it.

Drinks

Explain that tea comes from the leaves of the tea plant which have been dried and cut into small pieces. Ask children whose families use teabags to touch their nose. If possible show children some tea leaves and talk about these. Ask the children to think through the steps of making a cup of tea. What do they do first, what do they do last? Talk about the order being important. It's no good putting the water into the teapot before the tea!

Ask younger children to draw the stages of making a cup of tea and ask older children to write the stages.

Ask the children to tell you what other drinks they like and make a list of all these on the board. Read through the list and then ask them to bring in labels from these drinks or the cans so that you can look at the contents in the next activity.

Making tea

1. Put the kettle on first.
2. Get out the teapot and tea.
3. Get out the cups and saucers or mugs.
4. Put some milk in.
5. Warm the teapot.
6. Put in the tea or teabag.
7. Pour in the boiling water.
8. Leave to stand.
9. Pour out the tea carefully.

An average cup of tea contains around 60 mgs of caffeine, which is a mild stimulant. Ask older children to find out as much as they can about caffeine; what it is, what drinks contain it and how much is good or bad for us. See the fact sheet for teachers about caffeine in the appendix.

http://www.pe2000.com/caffeine.htm

What's in them?

Look at the labels that the children have brought in. Talk about the things that are in the drinks, such as sugar or sugar substitute, fruit – how much? flavourings, preservatives, caffeine. Explain the percentages by saying that, for example, 2% sugar means that if they had 100 cups of drink, two would be full of sugar.

Do any of the drinks mention calories? Do the children know what this word means? (Calories are the units of energy contained in the food and drink we consume. Calories are either burned to produce energy or, if excess to requirements, stored as fat.)

Do the children know that caffeine gives an energy boost? It is thought that drinks high in caffeine can make children hyperactive.

Bread

Talk about the different kinds of breads, from supermarket white sliced to granary whole grain. Ask the children which kind of bread they like and which they have in their homes. Jot down the kinds of breads they like to make a list and ask the children to 'vote with their feet' as to the kind they like best. (Choose different places in the room where children can stand to indicate their choice.) Count how many like each kind of bread.

Show the children your selection of different kinds of bread for them to taste. Cut it into thick slices and add a small amount of butter or margarine. Ask them again which bread they prefer. Have their preferences changed now that they have tasted different kinds of bread?

Do any of them know how to make bread? Do any of their parents make bread? Talk about yeast as a raising agent that gives the bread its little holes and makes it soft to eat. Talk about unleavened bread which has no raising agent.

You could visit the website: www.specialitybreads.co.uk/ and contact them to request a bread poster if you wish to use it to show the class.

Cream

Talk about cream teas that are popular in parts of this country, for example Cornish cream teas. Have any of the children had a cream tea? Remind them that these teas are usually scones with cream and jam. Ask the children to examine your collection of cream cartons and look at the amount of fat in each kind of cream. Are there any 'imitation' or 'low fat' creams there?

double, whipping, low fat, sour artificial and so on

Ask younger children to work in a group with each child choosing one cream pot to draw and to write alongside the amount of fat in 100 grams. Choose one of each kind of cream to make a class picture.

Ask older children to work in pairs to make a chart of the fat content in the various cartons of cream, using the 'per 100 grams' information. Ask them to put the one with the least fat at the top of their chart and the one with the most at the bottom.

Talk about cream being a treat, a food that is not really so good for our health but which we love to have on special occasions.

Jams and preserves

Explain to the children that all kinds of jams and marmalades used to be called 'preserves' because it was the only way of preserving fruit to eat out of season. In some countries 'mermalada' is the word for all kinds of jams. Ask the children if any of their families make jam or marmalade and if so ask them to tell the group how it is made, traditionally with as much sugar as fruit. Explain that boiling the fruit to soften it and lose some of the water content, then adding sugar and putting it into hot jars and sealing them stops the fruit from going bad. It preserves it. Years ago the only other way of preserving fruit was by bottling it – partly cooking it and putting it into special sealed jars.

Use the jam labels that the children have brought in. With younger children read out the fruit and sugar content of the various jams and compare them. What else is in the jams? Ask them to draw a picture of their favourite jar of jam and alongside it to draw the fruit(s) used to make it.

Ask older children to display the labels and work in groups to make a chart of the fruit, sugar and other contents from the contents lists on the various labels. They could use the activity sheet 'Jams and preserves'. They can also research preserves and jams (from books, families and the internet) and then write the recipe for one kind of jam.

Explain that now we have freezers most fruits can be preserved this way and that we can eat them out of season. Ask the children if they can tell you the seasons for UK fruit.

Sugar

Ask the children if they can tell you how we get sugar, which countries it grows in and how it is made from the plants. You could set older children this research task to do at home or school.

The children will already have seen that sugar is present in many foods as can be seen from looking at food packets.

Ask the children to think about what we use sugar for at home and what we add sugar to, such as drinks and fruit.

Ask them to finish the sentence, 'I add sugar to...

www.eatwell.gov.uk/healthydiet/foodmyths/ says:

'The sugars found naturally in whole fruit are less likely to cause tooth decay because the sugar is contained within the structure of the fruit. But, when fruit is juiced or blended, the sugar is released. Once released, these sugars can damage teeth, especially if fruit juice is drunk frequently.'

Have they mentioned putting it in pies, cakes, buns and biscuits and in preserves? Do they know there is a lot in sweets and chocolate?

Ask each child to draw somebody using sugar and to write what the person is doing. Explain that sugar and sugary foods can cause teeth to decay and that we should make sure we clean teeth twice a day, especially before going to bed after eating sugary foods.

Let's make it – biscuits

Make sure that you and the children wash hands before this activity.

Use the 1,2,3 recipe for biscuits; one part of sugar, two parts butter or margarine and three parts plain flour. You can flavour this mixture with spices, almond or vanilla essence and add dried fruit, chocolate bits or nuts. You may like the children to work in small groups, one group each day, with a different flavour for each day's biscuits.

With clean hands show the children how to mix the sugar and butter or margarine until it is smooth and then to add the flour and flavourings.

Show them how to bring the mixture together to form a long roll – like a sausage, and then to cut off slices to make rounds. (Older children could roll out the biscuit dough and cut rings of biscuits, but the previous method is easier for young children.) If you can bake these in the classroom all the children will benefit from the smell of the cooking. You could share each day's biscuits among all the children.

Let's make it – bread

Make sure that you and the children wash hands before this activity.

It is not difficult to make bread. Use strong flour (either plain, wholemeal or a half and half mixture) and follow the recipe on the flour packet. Explain that the yeast makes the dough rise and that the salt makes it stretchy and also inhibits yeast growth, that is, stops the yeast from making it rise too much.

You can make bread with the whole class in Circle Time if you ask selected children to help you with adding the yeast and mixing and pounding the dough. Leave it to rest under a cloth before coming together to knock it back and shape small rolls – one for each child.

Encourage them to 'play' with the dough and make interesting shapes, faces or animals for their rolls. This will help you to identify them after baking; it's a good idea also to mark them on baking tray in some way. Bake the bread in the classroom if you can. Sometimes the school cook will cook it. Share the rolls with a little spread while they are still a little warm.

Let's grow it – cress

Cress is very quick to grow – on a wet flannel or on some compost on a sunny windowsill. Time it to grow so you can eat it with the rolls you have made or, if not, with some of the bread you have brought in to show the children in the earlier activity.

Let's reflect and share

Remind the children that they have been learning about afternoon tea. You may like to have a tea party with some of the foods you have made. Remind the children of the kinds of fat that are good and that too much sugar is bad for teeth. Ask them to draw and write about this to take home to their families.

Ask the children to draw pictures of some healthy teatime foods and drinks to take home to share with their families. You could duplicate the fact sheet about sugar for them to take home for their families, together with any recipes for healthy teatime foods.

Jams and Preserves

My name is _____

Draw the pot and the label:	Write the contents:
	fruit..
	....
	sugar..
	....
	other contents:
	....
	....
	....
	....
	....
	Is there more fruit or more sugar?
	....
	....

Turn over the page and draw yourself enjoying eating your favourite jam or preserve. Write what it is and write about when you eat it.

Section 4: Evening Meal

In this section the children will be thinking about what they eat for their evening meal, after school or before they go to bed.

You will need packaging of foods that people eat at this meal as suggested in the homework section of 'The way in'.

Let's make it – toast

You will need a toaster and different kinds of bread in slices.

Let's make it – sardines, egg or beans on toast

You will need either a tin of sardines, tin of beans, some eggs or you may want all of these.

Let's grow it – salads

You will need seeds from:

- peppers
- cucumbers.

You can get these seeds from ripe fruits.

Suggested letter to parents and carers before starting work on this section

Dear Parents and Carers,

Evening meal

As part of our work on balanced eating we will be learning about and doing activities about the meal we eat at home at the end of the day. Some of you may call this tea and others may call it dinner. For the purpose of this work we will be calling it the evening meal.

We will be looking at the kinds of food and drink that people have for their evening meals. We'll be learning about different kinds of meats and poultry and about vegetarians who do not eat meat. We will be looking at different kinds of fish and fish dishes and the contents of fish meals.

The children will be learning about chocolate and where it comes from, that it is one of the 'treat' foods rather than part of everyday food and we'll be looking at foods we traditionally eat on toast. The children will be learning about and tasting fruit squashes.

We hope that you will show your child that you are interested in this topic and support them in this learning. If your child has any special dietary needs please make sure we know about them before we start this work.

Yours sincerely

Evening Meal

The way in...

In Circle Time remind the children that some people have their main meal of the day at noon and others in the evening. Ask them to think of the meal they have at home after school and before they go to bed. Ask them to raise a fist if they have a dinner meal, to put a thumb up if they have a teatime kind of meal, to touch their shoulders if they have a hot snack, such as beans on toast for their evening meal.

Ask the children to finish the sentence: 'Yesterday for my evening meal I had…' Jot down on the board what the children say to make a list. When all the children have finished, read the list aloud and talk about each food and drink. Ask those who also like each food to touch their nose.

Yesterday we had…

beans on toast
curry
pizza
jerk chicken and rice
fish and chips
omelette
sandwiches
cake
ice cream
banana
milk
hot chocolate.

Ask volunteers to say whether they choose what they have to eat or whether they have to have what the rest of the family will be eating and drinking. Does the family all eat together or do the children eat at a different time? Do they sit at a table or sit in front of the TV? Is it different at weekends? Talk about who makes this evening meal. Does one of the grown-ups make it or do the children help? What can the children do to help? Who does the washing-up?

Talk about chips. Ask children who like chips to stand up. Is everyone standing? Explain that chips taste really good, but are deep fried in fat. Talk about fish. Ask children to stand up if they like fish. Ask these children the kinds of fish they like – are they fish like you get from the fish and chip shop or do some children have differently cooked fish?

Before ending the Circle Time session ask the children to close their eyes and think of a balanced evening meal they would like to have today, one without too much fat, sugar or salt. Ask them to make a picture in their heads of this meal and tell them that you will want them to draw this picture later.

Homework

Ask the children to bring in any tins or their labels from any of their evening meal foods. Ask them to jot down the names of these foods. Ask them to bring in the cleaned outer packaging or labels from all kinds of fish products.

Younger Children

Draw and Talk

Ask the children to draw the picture of themselves having their balanced evening meal. Ask them to draw the foods that are in this really healthy meal. Ask them to draw a healthy drink to go with the meal.

As the children finish their pictures ask them to come to you (or the classroom helper) in a quiet place to talk about their picture.

As each child tells you about their picture write keywords of foods in a corner of the picture.

Ask each child these three prompt questions:

1. What foods have you drawn for this meal?

2. What drinks have you drawn for this meal?

3. Which of the foods you have drawn do you think will be the best at helping you to grow up well and healthy?

cheese
egg
salad
bread and butter
chocolate biscuit
apple
drink of water.

I think all these are really healthy foods, not the chocolate biscuit. Water is healthy.

Then ask each child how she feels when she is eating this really healthy meal. Take the drawings to the next Circle Time and ask the children if you can show their pictures to everyone and read out the things they have said.

Talk about the things they have drawn. Do the children agree that all these things are good for them? Are some of them really treats? Are some of these things 'home made'? Are some of these foods made in shops and frozen? Have some of the children drawn packets of crisps and other similar foods? How many have drawn chips?

Count up the number of children who have drawn fish, vegetables, fruit, fruit juice, water. Ask for a show of hands from children who like to eat these things. Praise those children who mentioned water telling them that this is the healthiest drink of all.

Older Children

Draw and Write

Explain the rules for Draw and Write, to use their own ideas without sharing them and without talking about what they are drawing. Remind them to be ready to stop drawing and start the writing when asked and:

- not to worry about spellings

- to ask the scribe in a whisper to write what they say if they need help

- to go back to finish their drawing when they have written all they can.

> I drew pasta with a lot of cheese sauce. I will have a banana. I like pasta and bananas; they are healthy. I choose my evening meal. I feel happy because Mum makes food I like.

Ask the children to think about the picture they made in their heads in Circle Time. Then ask them to fold their paper in half and on one half to draw this picture of themselves having this balanced evening meal.

After the children have had a few minutes to draw, stop them and ask them to write on the other half of the paper about:

- what healthy food they have drawn

- what healthy drink they have drawn

- who chooses their evening meal.

As the children are writing, walk around the class and remind them of the things you asked them to write about.

When all the children have finished their drawing and writing, ask them to join you in a group or circle to talk about what they have drawn and written and their feelings about their evening mealtime. How many of the children have drawn vegetables? How many have drawn fruit or fruit juice? How many drew water to drink? Talk about the foods and drinks that the children think are healthy. Do all the children agree about this?

Talking about and sharing what the children have drawn and written is a vital part of this work. You may like to use some of the pictures and writing to make a display.

Activities

Additives and preservatives

Tell the children that when foods are made in factories, whether they are frozen or fresh, they have to have things called 'preservatives' to make sure that the foods will last for a few days and won't go bad. Tell them that some foods have 'additives', artificial things that have to be added to make the food look the right colour and taste the way it should. Explain that these things often have numbers that sometimes begin with the letter E and so are called 'E numbers'. Say that fresh foods cooked at home do not need these things adding to them. Talk about 'fresh' and what it means; food freshly picked or freshly bought, not foods that have been in the fridge, fruit bowl or vegetable rack for many days. Frozen and tinned foods can be very fresh because they are usually frozen or tinned the day they are harvested. Explain that we tend to think of 'fresh foods' as those that are freshly picked and eaten straight away.

Ask younger children to draw a picture of three kinds of food; a tin of food, some frozen food and some fresh food. Ask them to label their drawings and give their picture a title.

Ask older children to look at the labels from tins that they have brought in. Tell them to work in pairs and find out the additives and preservatives in those foods and to make a list of them. Come together as a class and look at what the children have found out. Ask each pair to choose one type of tinned food, for example, soup, and make a computerised list of contents from all the labels on those tins, each with the additives and preservatives listed alongside. You may like to display their lists with a suitable heading and with comments from the children in speech bubbles around the list saying which foods have the most and least of these additions.

You could do the same activity with frozen foods.

Meat

See www.bmesonline.org.uk/s_resources.htm for free resources.

You may wish to avoid the following two activities with the youngest children but older children do need to know where their food comes from.

Ask the children which meats they like, writing up on the board the words beef, pork, lamb, mutton and venison. Count up and write the numbers of children who like each alongside.

Talk about the different animals that provide us with meat. Write on the board the words, bull and cow, pig and sow, sheep and ram, buck and doe (deer and rabbit) and explain that these are the names of the male and female animals.

Explain that there are different names for most animals and their meat and ask the children if they know which meat comes from which animal. Write these on the board. Join the animal word to the meat word using a coloured line. Which meats have the same name as the animal? (lamb, rabbit).

Explain that we call these meats 'red meat'. Explain that some people prefer not to eat red meat because of the fat, but meat is a healthy part of our food as it contains things that help our bodies to be healthy. Tell children that even if you cut off the fat there is still some fat in the meat. Ask the children to complete the activity sheet 'Meats'. (Vegetarians can omit the word 'meat' on the turn over activity.)

Make a class picture of farm animals, asking the children to draw and cut out pictures of the animals to paste onto a field background. Ask older children to write about these animals and the meat they give.

Poultry

Ask the children if they know what poultry is. If not explain that this is the meat that we get from birds that have been farmed to provide people with meat. Write the names on the board for the different kinds of poultry such as chicken, turkey, goose, duck and say that we use the names of these birds for the bird itself and for the meat it gives us.

Tell the children that chicken and turkey meat contain very little fat and that some people prefer to eat these instead of red meat because of this.

Ask the children to draw pictures of these farmed birds to add to their class picture of farm animals.

Vegetarians

Explain that some people do not eat meat either because they don't like it or because they don't like the thought of eating animals. Explain that these people are called vegetarians. Tell the children that people who don't eat meats have to make sure that they eat plenty of foods such as eggs, cheese, beans and grains so that their bodies will still be healthy.

Ask the children to think of a meal that they like that doesn't have meat in it. Ask volunteers to say what these meals are. Ask them all to choose and draw a balanced meal with no meat or poultry but with vegetables and other foods. Ask them to name the foods they have drawn and ask older children to write about this meal.

Fish

Make a poster

Ask children to work in pairs to visit www.fishonline.org. Click 'search', then type in the name of the fish you want to see. To print the picture, right click.

Ask the children to choose a few of the fish they like, know or want to know more about and to download pictures and data about these fish. Ask them to make a poster using the information from the data they have collected and the pictures which they can print, cut out and display on their poster. Ask them to add their own information, perhaps in the form of speech bubbles about whether:

- they like to eat the various species of fish

- they have seen them in fishmonger's shops

- these are protected and rare species

- they live in waters around the UK or elsewhere.

Fish we know

cod
hake
sardines
salmon
trout
haddock
kippers
tuna.

Display the posters on tables or walls for all the children to see each other's work. Discuss the posters and ask them to vote on the few you can more permanently display.

Ask the children to raise an elbow if they like to eat fish. Do they know where fish come from and where they are caught? Do any of their parents go fishing? Have the children ever gone fishing with them? If so, ask these children to tell the others about it.

Do the children know about fish farms? Explain how these work and that the fish are fed food pellets and kept in huge ponds or enormous cages in water. Tell them that wild fish taste better than farmed fish because they are freer to swim longer distances and have to catch their own food.

Ask them to think of the names of any fish they eat and to finish the sentence: 'A fish I like to eat is...' Jot down the names of these fish and ask the children if they know what these fish look like. Talk about the ways these fish are cooked and how we eat them.

Talk about where you go to buy fish to eat. Is there a fishmonger where the children can see fish displayed? Does a local supermarket have a fish counter? Perhaps you could take some of the children in small groups to look at the different kinds of fish.

Look at the outer packaging of fish products that the children have brought in. Some of these will have contained whole fish, raw or cooked, some filleted or coated; some will be minced fish with other ingredients. With younger children talk about the amount of fish in each product. Talk about what else is in the product and make a list on the board. Talk about which has the most fish and which has the least.

Ask older children to work in pairs or small groups to investigate the contents on the labels of the packaging and make a chart of their findings. These should include the amount of fish in each product and all the other ingredients. Discuss their charts as a whole class.

Cooking foods

Talk to the children about the ways we cook food at home. Explain that there are several ways to cook foods but that they all involve heating the food to a great heat and making sure that the food is cooked all the way through.

Ask the children if they can think of some of the ways we cook fish. Ask volunteers to tell the group and make a list on the board. Then repeat this activity with meat, cheese, eggs and vegetables.

Ask any children who can, to describe these ways of cooking food. Explain the ways that the children cannot describe and add to their list with ways of cooking that they do not offer.

Explain that we can overcook foods and that this takes away some of the goodness, for example, vegetables should just be cooked a short time until they are just a little soft and not boiled for a long time. Explain that a healthy way to cook vegetables is by steaming; that if people boil them the water in which they are boiled is called stock and can be used to make tasty soups or gravy.

Cooking

frying
poaching
boiling
steaming
slow cooking
in the oven
in a pot with liquid
grilling
microwaving
on a barbecue.

Grilling or stir frying are healthy ways of cooking some kinds of meats and poultry; it is healthy because very little, if any, fat is used this way.

Ask the children to draw someone in their family cooking some food in one of these ways and to label their drawings or write a few sentences about the food and the way it is cooked.

Chocolate

Ask the children to raise a hand if they like chocolate and chocolate puddings. Ask them to put up a thumb if they like drinking chocolate or cocoa. Count and display these numbers. Are they 100%? Ask them if they know where chocolate comes from and ask those who do to tell the group. Are they correct? Explain that chocolate has a lot of fat and sugar and because of this it is not healthy to eat too much of it. It should be eaten as treats, not a regular part of their daily food.

How chocolate is made

Before the lesson you might like to visit www.cadbury.co.uk/EN/CTB2003/ about_chocolate and find your way around it.

The website has a learning zone, at present being redeveloped, as well as an order form for resources for Key Stages 1-4.

Show young children how to click on 'making chocolate' where they can see pictures of cocoa trees and beans which they can print. Ask pairs of children to make an A4 information sheet about how chocolate is made using the pictures which they can print, cut out and stick on their paper. Help the youngest children to write a sentence about their pictures; those who can write for themselves can add their own writing.

Ask older children to work in pairs or small groups to investigate the whole site. Ask them to write a small four page pamphlet about how chocolate is made by folding an A3 sheet in half. They will need to design a front cover with title and authorship. Tell them to use the inside and back pages for information and pictures which they can find on the website as well as from books from your school library. (You could set this as 'homework' if all your children have home computers.)

Drinks

You will need a bottle of squash, water, four jugs and some cups for this activity. Ask the children to tell you all the drinks they like. Ask them to finish the sentence, 'I like… to drink', with each child contributing one drink. Make a list. Ask anyone who repeats a drink to change places with the person who last said it. When everyone has had a turn look at the list. Is water there? If not add it.

Read out each drink in turn and ask the children to raise a hand if they like it, adding the number of children who like it alongside the name of the drink.

Examine your bottle of squash, looking for the amount of fruit juice and sugar as well as additives and preservatives. Talk about these. Read what the instructions say about the dilution of the drink. Ask the children to watch while you dilute the squash according to the instructions in one of the jugs. Dilute the squash with half as much water again in the second jug and dilute it with twice as much water for the third jug. In the fourth jug pour just water.

Ask each child to taste each drink and note down which they like the best and which they like the least. At the end of the day come together as a class and talk about which drinks they like best and least. Ask which drink they think is the healthiest. Remind children about the additives and preservatives. How many of them prefer water? Remind them that water is the healthiest drink of all.

Ask older children to examine any bottles of squash they have at home. Ask them to write down the name of the squash, the name of the fruit and the contents as listed on the label and bring this to school. Talk about these as a whole class, discussing which squash they prefer and why.

Let's make it – toast

Make sure that you and the children wash hands before this activity.

Toast is easy to make in the classroom using a toaster. Use different kinds of bread. Each group could choose to make sufficient for a quarter slice per child. You could let them butter their own and add marmalade, honey or jam, according to their taste.

Let's make it – sardines, egg or beans on toast

Make sure that you and the children wash hands before this activity.

Having made the toast as before, mash sardines with a little vinegar or lemon juice, warm beans or cook scrambled egg in a microwave. If you use about six slices of toast you could add various toppings, cut them into very small pieces and let the children taste a variety of these snacks. Ask the children which they prefer. Will all the children taste each one?

Let's grow it – salads

Grow fruits such as peppers, courgettes or cucumbers in the classroom. You don't need to buy seeds; you can use the seeds from a ripe red pepper, courgette or cucumber. Ask the children to plant these in small pots, transferring them to larger pots as they grow. With care and attention these will fruit in pots on a classroom windowsill.

Let's reflect and share

Remind the children that they have been learning about evening meals and food cooked at home.

Ask the children to share what they have learned with their family at home. Perhaps they can take the chocolate fact sheet home, together with their work about additives and preservatives. If you have made a display about their work you could invite parents to come and look at it.

Remind them that all food is good for them but some foods are healthier and will help to make them grow up healthy and well.

Meat

Draw the animals:

Beef	Pork
The male animal is a	The male animal is a ....
The female is a..............................	The female is a..............................
Lamb	**Venison**
The male animal is a	The male animal is a ....
The female is a..............................	The female is a..............................

I like to eat................................. best. We eat this when................................

....

....

**Turn over the page and draw a picture of you and your family having a meal
with meat. Write about your picture.**

Section 5: Barbecues

In this section the children will be thinking about what they eat at a barbecue and how some of these foods are prepared.

Let's make it – vegetable kebabs

You'll need wooden skewers, olive oil, a small brush and a selection of vegetables.

Let's make it – salad dressing

You'll need

- garlic (if liked)

- 1 rounded teaspoon of dry mustard

- 1 tablespoon of vinegar

- little black pepper

- 6 tablespoons olive oil.

Let's grow it – lettuce

You'll need

- a packet of lettuce seed

- yoghurt pots of soil or soil compound

- a larger seed tray of soil compound and a dibber

- pots or a garden for final planting.

Suggested letter to parents and carers before starting work on this section

Dear Parents and Carers

Barbecues

As part of our work on balanced eating we will be learning about and doing activities about the food we eat at barbecues. These are becoming more and more popular and children enjoy eating out of doors.

We will be looking at the kinds of food and drink that people have at barbecues. We'll be learning about the contents of various sausages and beefburgers and any additives and preservatives in these.

We will be talking about what happens to rubbish and about composting vegetable waste to use in the garden. If you have compost bins you could help by letting the children help you to use them. If not, and you have a garden, you may like to take this opportunity to start a compost bin. The children may bring home a fact sheet about composting.

We hope that you will show your child that you are interested in this work and support them while they are doing this project. If your child has any special dietary needs please make sure we know about them before we start.

Yours sincerely

Barbecues

The way in...

In Circle Time start by talking about your outdoor eating and barbecues. Describe a barbecue that you have been to and tell the children how it was organised.

Ask the children to touch their ears if they have been to a barbecue. Have any of them not been to a barbecue?

Ask the children to finish the sentence: 'When I go to a barbecue I like to eat...' Jot down on the board what the children say to make a list. When all the children have finished, read the list to them and talk about the different foods.

Ask volunteers to say what they like to drink at barbecues and make a list of these drinks.

At barbecues we like to eat...

sausages
chops
mushrooms
kebabs
steak
beefburgers
chicken
salads
bread
garlic bread.

Remind the children that barbecues get very hot and ask them how they make sure they stay safe by keeping away from them. Talk about the things that grown-ups have to have and to do to make sure they don't burn themselves. Talk about when and where people have barbecues. Ask them to tell you whether they have theirs in their garden, do they have them on holiday or on camp sites? Do they go to barbecue parties at other people's houses? What do they do if it starts to rain?

Before ending the Circle Time session ask the children to close their eyes and think of going to a special barbecue. Ask them to make a picture in their heads of this barbecue and tell them that you will want them to draw this picture later.

Homework

Ask the children to bring in cleaned wrappings from sausages, beefburgers and other barbecue meat packs that show what is in them. Collect these to use later.

Younger Children

Draw and Talk

Ask the children to draw the picture of themselves at the barbecue. Ask them to draw all the foods that they like to eat and drink there. Ask them to colour in any barbecue foods that they think are really good for helping them to grow up well and healthy.

As the children finish their pictures ask them to come to you (or the classroom helper) in a quiet place to talk about their picture.

As each child tells you about their picture write keywords of foods in a corner of the picture.

Ask each child these four prompt questions:

1.   What will you eat at this barbecue?

2.   What will you drink there?

3.   Where is this barbecue?

4.   What are you doing to keep safe there?

Barbecue

sausages
garlic bread
kebabs
salad

The barbecue is in my garden. My dad has tongs to hold the hot food. I am keeping safe by not going too near the barbecue.

Take the drawings to the next Circle Time and ask the children if you can show their pictures to everyone and read out the things they have said.

Talk about all the foods that the children have drawn and talked about. Find out what the children most like to eat at barbecues and add to the list you made in 'The way in' activity and count the numbers of children who like each food.

Talk about all the different kinds of meats that they barbecue, for example, sausages, burgers, kebabs or chops. Talk about the kinds of shops that sell meat, for example, a butcher's shop, a farmers' market, a supermarket or freezer shop.

Start to make a class picture of a barbecue. Enlist the children's help in preparing the background and ask them to draw figures to paste on or use some of their Draw and Talk pictures. (If you want to keep their original pictures you could photocopy some for the class picture.) Ask the children to suggest comments to write on speech bubbles to go around the picture. Add your own questions. Ask the children to think of a title.

Older Children

Draw and Write

Explain the rules for Draw and Write, to use their own ideas without sharing them and without talking about what they are drawing. Remind them to be ready to stop drawing and start the writing when asked and:

- not to worry about spellings

- to ask the scribe in a whisper to write what they say if they need help

- to go back to finish their drawing when they have written all they can.

Ask the children to think about the picture they made in their heads in Circle Time. Then ask them to fold their paper in half and on one half to draw this picture of themselves at the barbecue. Ask them to draw all the foods that they like to eat at a barbecue. Ask them to draw the drinks that will be there.

After the children have had a few minutes to draw, stop them and ask them to write on the other half of the paper about:

There are all kinds of meats on the barbecue and vegetable kebabs. There is wine and beer to drink for grown-ups. I am eating sausages and mushrooms and kebabs and drinking coke. I love barbecues and my friends are there.

- what there is to eat at this barbecue

- what there is to drink there

- what they will choose to eat and drink

- how they are feeling at the barbecue.

As the children are writing, walk around the class and remind them of the things you asked them to write about.

When all the children have finished their drawing and writing, ask them to join you in a group or circle to talk about what they have drawn and written and their feelings about barbecues. Investigate what the children have drawn and make a list of the popular barbecue foods. Analyse what the children said they would drink and make a chart of the findings.

Talking about and sharing what the children have drawn and written is a vital part of this work. You may like to use some of the pictures and writing to add to your class picture.

Activities

Sausages

Ask the children to tell you the name of the person who sells meat. Explain that a butcher means 'a person who deals in meat'. Ask older children to use a dictionary to find out other ways that the words 'to butcher' are used.

Talk about how sausages are made. Can the children tell you? Explain that some people make their own sausages at home by putting lean meats in a food processor and adding herbs, seasonings and sometimes vegetables or apple. Sometimes they put them in skins, but often home made sausages are just shaped in flour and then cooked.

Explain that butchers usually make their own sausages. Sometimes they use animal parts for the skins and sometimes they use other edible skins. Tell the children that butcher's sausages and home made sausages taste quite different from those from supermarkets because they do not need to add preservatives and additives as they are freshly made for people to buy that day and take home to cook immediately.

Ask the younger children if they know what meats are usually put into sausages (beef and pork) and explain that these are usually off cuts or bits of meat that would be too small for butchers to sell on their own.

Talk about organic meat (see fact sheet on organics in the appendix).

Beef burgers

Explain that beef burgers are made from beef that has been minced up and that sometimes there are other things added to make them taste better. Some people make their own beef burgers with meat and onion; these do not need additives. Do any of their families make their own beef burgers?

Ask the children to stand up if they like beef burgers. Count them; is all the class standing? If any remain sitting ask them to tell you why they don't like them. Ask volunteers to say where they like to eat their beef burgers and make a list of the places they mention. Ask them how often they eat beef burgers and whether they think these are healthy foods or treat foods.

Packaging

With younger children, examine the packaging from beef burgers and sausages that they have brought in and talk about the meat and fat content. Are the children surprised at how much meat and fat are the packs? What else is in them? Talk about additives and preservatives in these foods. Explain that it is necessary to add some of these so that the foods do not go bad, but that some additives are there to make them taste better and may not always be very good for us if we eat a lot of them.

Ask older children to examine the cleaned wrappers from packs of sausages and beef burgers that they have brought in. Ask them to work in pairs or groups to look at the meat and fat content of both sausages and beef burgers and to make a chart of their findings. Talk about what they find out. Is there a lot of difference between different packs? Are they surprised at how much or how little meat is in these packs? Explain about percentages, for example, by saying that 20% fat means that if they could separate the fat from the meat and cut the food into 100 equal portions, 20 of the portions would be all fat; if they cut them into 10 portions, two would be all fat and if they cut them into five portions one would be all fat.

Breads

Talk about the kinds of breads we have at a barbecue. Ask volunteers to say what kinds of bread they like to eat with a barbecue and make a list of these.

Talk about the breads that the children like best and which they like least. Ask the children to think which one bread they like very best and to 'vote with their feet' by going to stand in a certain place in the classroom to indicate their choice.

(There are more activities about bread in the next section.)

> **Barbecue breads**
>
> long rolls
> round rolls
> French stick bread
> garlic bread
> sliced loaf
> white bread
> granary
> wholemeal.

Salads

Ask the children to help you to make a list of all the things we can have in a salad. Write all these on the board. Talk about those that are vegetables, leaves, fruits and stems. Explain that fruits come after a flower has died, so tomatoes and peppers are really fruits; sometimes we eat the roots (potatoes, carrots) or stems (celery) and leaves (lettuce).

Ask the children if any can tell you how salad crops are grown. Remind them that some grow above the ground and some grow under the ground. Look at your list and draw a purple ring around those that grow under the ground. Explain that we call these root vegetables and these have to be washed very carefully to get all the soil off them before they are eaten.

Talk about the others, those that grow above the ground. Explain that these can have soil and small creatures around them so that they, too, need to be carefully washed before they are eaten.

Talk about supermarkets and shops that have packets of washed salads. These can be on the shelves for some days; they are kept fresh by a special gas that stops them from going bad so quickly. They may not be as newly harvested as those bought from a greengrocer. Explain that the freshest vegetables are the healthiest as these still have nutrients in them that get lost when vegetables are stored.

Ask the children if any of their families grow vegetables and ask any volunteers to talk about what they grow. Explain that freshly grown vegetables and salads are really good for us, especially if they are grown organically.

Read, with the children, the list you made on the board. Use the activity sheet 'Salads' and ask the children to draw the salad foods you have listed on your board in the correct columns. Ask older children to add writing about each salad food and to write which they like and why.

Organic vegetables

Tell the children that commercial growers of vegetables and salad crops use chemicals to kill insects that like to eat the crop and sprays that help the crop to grow. Many people do not like to eat food that has been sprayed and so some farmers grow vegetables and salads organically. This means no chemicals in their sprays, just natural things that won't harm the pests. They put natural goodness back into the soil, such as garden or vegetable waste. See the fact sheet in the appendix for more information. See also the website http://www.hdra.org.uk/

Composting

Explain to the children that most of the rubbish that is collected from our houses goes into big holes in the ground which is then covered over with soil. This is bad for the world but there is no-where else for it to go unless we can recycle it. Explain that recycling garden and household vegetable waste is a good way to put goodness back into the soil as well as making less rubbish to go in landfill sites.

Ask the children if they have a garden and whether they have a compost bin. If any do, ask them to explain what goes into the bin and what comes out of it. See the fact sheet in the appendix for more information.

Olive oil

Before barbecuing food, meats and vegetables are usually brushed with a little oil. In the past many people used to use animal fats for cooking chips and frying eggs and other foods, but nowadays most people use oils. Ask volunteers to talk about the oils that their parents use for cooking. Tell them that there are several kinds of oils and that they are all good for us. Olive oil is one of the really healthy oils that we use for cooking.

Ask volunteers to say if they know where olive oil comes from. Explain that it comes from a tree that grows in warm countries. The olive fruit is a small fleshy fruit which starts off being green and turns black as it ripens. Ask children if they like olives and on what food they have olives. Tell them that you can use olive oil for making mayonnaise.

Tell the children that olive oil is made from pressing the olives and collecting the oil that runs out of the presses. The first pressing is a very thick rich oil, greenish in colour and many people like this a lot and pay more money for this. It is called virgin oil. The olives are pressed over and over again until all the oil has been collected and then what is left of the olives is used as fertiliser on the land. See the fact sheet in the appendix for more information.

Salad creams and dressings

Tell the children that olive and other oils are used to make mayonnaise and salad dressings. Mayonnaise is made from oil, vinegar and raw eggs with flavourings such as herbs and mustard. Ask if any of the children have seen their families make mayonnaise. It is easy to make (especially if you have a blender) by mixing an egg yolk with lemon juice or vinegar before drizzling in the oil gradually as the blender is working. You can add herbs, mustard or garlic when it is mixed. (The name comes from Mahon in Minorca where it was first made in 1756. The chef, preparing for a feast was going to make a special sauce from cream and eggs but there was no cream so he substituted olive oil for the cream and created Mahonnaise.)

Many people do not like to use home made mayonnaise these days as they do not like to eat uncooked eggs, which could be infected. Salad dressings are usually made from olive oil and vinegar or lemon juice with some flavourings such as herbs, garlic and mustard. Ask children if they have ever helped to do this.

Let's make it – salad dressing

Make sure that you and the children wash hands before this activity.

You'll need a few small bottles or jars with tops – one for each group as well as the ingredients. You can use malt vinegar; but balsamic or wine vinegar are better. Put the crushed garlic in the jar with the dry ingredients, put

The basic recipe is:

1 rounded teaspoon of dry mustard
1 tablespoon of vinegar
little black pepper
6 tablespoons olive oil.
$\frac{1}{2}$ clove garlic (if liked).

on the top and shake about until they are mixed. Add the vinegar and shake; add the oil slowly and keep shaking.

Let's make it – vegetable kebabs

Make sure that you and the children wash hands before this activity.

Bring in some wooden skewers, olive oil, small brush and a selection of some or all of the following vegetables:

courgettes
mushrooms – different kinds
tomatoes – large
peppers – red and yellow
onion
herbs.

Show the children how to cut the vegetables and thread them onto the skewers. Even young children can do this if they are shown how to do it carefully and if the knives are sharp enough. Brush the vegetables with the olive oil and add any herbs if you wish. You can cook these under a grill, in an oven or ask the school cook to put them in their oven.

Allow them to cool and eat them outside if it's a sunny day.

Let's grow it – lettuce

You'll need a packet of lettuce seed for this. Show the children how to sprinkle a few seeds onto the top of a yoghurt pot of soil or soil compound. Water, and put on a sunny windowsill until the seeds are large enough to handle. You'll need a larger seed tray of soil compost and a dibber to make the holes. Show the children how to transplant the seeds – holding the leaf of each plantlet and not touching the roots. Put the seed tray in a sunny place and water. When the plants are large enough transfer them, either one to a plant pot to grow inside or into an outside bed. You could let children take theirs home to plant in their garden or eat some with the salad dressing.

Let's reflect and share

Remind the children that they have been learning about barbecues and the kinds of food we eat there. Can they now tell you what a healthily balanced barbecue meal would be?

Remind them that no food is bad for them, but that some foods are healthier for them than others and that foods that are not so healthy can be used as treats.

Salads

My name is _____

Draw the foods in the right place and write their names.

We eat these leaves:	We eat these fruits:
We eat these stems:	We eat these roots:

Turn over the page and draw a picture of yourself eating a salad. What kinds of foods do you like to have in your salad? Write about them.

Section 6: Picnics

In this section the children will be thinking about picnics and outdoor eating, what they eat and drink on a picnic and how some of these foods are prepared.

You will need a photocopy of the British Isles for each pair of children for the cheese activity.

Let's make it – cream cheese

You'll need

- old creamy milk
- glass bowl or dish
- muslin for straining.

Let's make it – pizzas

See the recipe on page 98.

Let's make it – sandwiches

You'll need

- slices of different kinds of bread
- cream cheese
- various other fillings.

Let's grow it – tomatoes

You'll need

- a packet of tomato seed or some seeds from a ripe tomato.

Suggested letter to parents and carers before starting work on this section

Dear Parents and Carers

Picnics

As part of our work on balanced eating we will be learning about and doing activities about the food and drink we take on a picnic.

We'll be learning about and tasting various cheeses and hope to make some for ourselves. We'll be making pizzas to eat in the classroom.

Part of this work is concerned with looking at picnic containers and recycling plastic bags. We hope that you will let your children convince you of the need to re-use these and then recycle them.

We hope that you will show your child that you are interested in this work and support them while they are doing this project. If your child has any special dietary needs please make sure we know about them before we start.

Yours sincerely,

Picnics

The way in...

In Circle Time start by talking about a picnic you have been on. Tell the children about where you went, the things you did, ate and drank. Ask them to think about a picnic they have been on – perhaps a school outing. Ask the children to finish the sentence: 'I went on a picnic to...' Jot down on the board what the children say to make a list. When all the children have finished, read the list to them and talk about all the different places where we can go to have a picnic.

> **Picnics**
>
> at the seaside
> the park
> the country
> on holiday
> on a campsite
> my garden
> on a journey
> on a boat
> the woods
> a beauty spot
> a national park
> the New Forest.

Ask the children to tell you what else they take with them on a picnic. Perhaps they take something to sit on, something to play with, something to keep the hot sun off them.

Talk to the children about the food we have on picnics. Ask volunteers to tell you their favourite picnic food and talk about who makes the picnic food – do they help?

Talk about the things we drink on picnics. Do their families take hot drinks? Do they make a hot drink at the picnic? How do they do this? Do they take flasks of drink or do they have cold drinks?

Talk about some picnic foods as being treats, when we have foods and drinks that are perhaps not quite so healthy for a treat.

Before ending the Circle Time session ask the children to close their eyes and think of a time when they went on a picnic and what they had to eat and drink there. Ask them to make a picture in their heads of this picnic and tell them that you will want them to draw this picture later.

Homework

Ask younger children to look in magazines and try to find and cut out pictures of people on picnics. Ask them to bring pictures of the picnic food and drink and all the things that people take with them on a picnic.

Ask all children to look for and bring to school pictures of cheeses and cheese packaging from cheese they have at home.

Younger Children

Draw and Talk

Ask the children to draw the picture of themselves on this picnic sitting down and eating and drinking picnic food. Ask them to draw all the foods that they like to eat and drink on a picnic. Ask them to colour any foods that they think are really good for helping them to grow up well and healthy.

As the children finish their pictures ask them to come to you (or the classroom helper) in a quiet place to talk about their picture.

As each child tells you about their picture write keywords of foods in a corner of the picture.

Ask each child these four prompt questions:

1. Where are you on this picnic?

2. Who is with you on this picnic?

3. What foods and drinks would you like to take with you on this picnic?

4. What would you not take on a picnic?

Take the drawings to the next Circle Time and ask the children if you can show their pictures to everyone and read out the things they have said.

Picnic

sandwiches
hard boiled eggs
meat pie
yogurt
an apple
a drink of orange.

I am in the forest with my mum and sister. I would not take chocolate biscuits because they would melt.

Talk about the most popular picnic foods and make a list of these. Ask the children to tell you which they think are especially healthy and which are treats.

Talk about what they have said they would like to drink and make a list. Are these all healthy drinks or are some of them treats? Draw a red circle around the treat drinks.

Talk about the things they would not take with them and ask the children to say why these things are not good picnic foods and drinks.

Make a large class picture of a picnic at the seaside. Enlist the children's help with the background and ask them all to draw themselves sitting at a picnic meal. Add playthings such as buckets and spades, sun umbrellas and other seaside toys. Add your own questions. Ask the children to think of a title.

Older Children

Draw and Write

Explain the rules for Draw and Write, to use their own ideas without sharing them and without talking about what they are drawing. Remind them to be ready to stop drawing and start the writing when asked and:

- not to worry about spellings

- to ask the scribe in a whisper to write what they say if they need help

- to go back to finish their drawing when they have written all they can.

Ask the children to think about the picture they made in their heads in Circle Time. Then ask them to fold their paper in half and on one half to draw this picture of themselves having a picnic with their family and friends.

After the children have had a few minutes to draw, stop them and ask them to write on the other half of the paper about:

I am in the garden with my friends. Dad made the picnic tea. We are having cheese flan and wraps to eat and squash and fruit. I am feeling hot and happy with my friends on this picnic.

- the people who are sharing this picnic

- who made the picnic food

- their favourite picnic foods and drinks

- how they are feeling as they having their picnic.

As the children are writing, walk around the class and remind them of the things you asked them to write about.

When all the children have finished their drawing and writing, ask them to join you in a group or circle to talk about what they have drawn and written and their feelings about picnics. How many of the children have drawn fruit, fruit juice or yoghurt? How many drew a canned drink? Did any draw water? Talk about which foods and drinks the children think are the healthiest and which are not so healthy.

Talking about and sharing what the children have drawn and written is a vital part of this work. You may like to use some of the pictures and writing to make a display.

Activities

Picnics

For younger children. Look at the pictures the children have brought about picnics, picnic foods and drinks and containers. Talk about all the things in the pictures. Talk about the places where the picnics are. Ask volunteers to tell you about a picnic they have been to. Can the children cut out and use their pictures to make a picture of a picnic?

Sandwiches

Talk to the children about the kinds of sandwiches they like. Ask volunteers to say what kinds of bread or cover they like and the fillings they prefer.

Ask them to suggest more fillings and make a list of these on the board. Ask children which are their favourite fillings for sandwiches and write the numbers alongside.

Talk about the different kinds of outsides that can be used to make kinds of sandwiches, for example, rolls, pitta bread or wraps.

Ask the youngest children which story book character liked marmalade sandwiches and ask them to draw a picture of Paddington Bear eating his marmalade sandwiches.

Sandwich fillings
egg 10
cheese and tomato 7
chicken 15
cheese and pickle 4
tuna 2
lettuce and tomato 8
sardine 1
meat and pickle 5
jam 19
marmalade 2
marmite 3

Ask older children to find out about Lord Sandwich who is thought to have 'invented' sandwiches. Where and when did he do this? Talk about other people who have given their names to things in everyday use, for example, Wellington, Cardigan. Ask them to find out about these people for homework.

UK cheeses

For older children, you'll need a duplicated map of the UK, one for each pair of children.

British cheeses
Caerphilly
Cheddar
Cheshire
Double Gloucester
Lancashire
Lymeswold
Red Leicester
Stilton
Wensleydale
West Country farmhouse.

Look at the pictures of cheese and cheese wrappers that the children have brought in.

Write their names on the board. Explain that many areas of the UK have cheeses that are special to the area.

How many different kinds of UK cheese have the children brought in? Can the children tell you some more? Add these names to the list and draw a ring around the UK cheeses.

Ask older children to use the map of the UK, work in pairs and find the places (counties) where all the cheeses they know are made. Ask them to colour in or draw a picture of cheese on these place names.

Make a poster

Use the website www.cheese.com where there are pictures and information about any number of cheeses. Type in the name of any cheese (and spelling doesn't matter) and up will come a picture of the cheese and some information about it. This website also gives information about cheese by country and cheese facts.

Ask younger children to work in pairs find out about one cheese on the website, print the picture and help them to use the information to write a sentence about that kind of cheese. You can put all these on a poster for everyone to share.

Set older children the task of finding out about cheeses from different countries by asking each group of, say eight, children to choose one country to find out about the cheeses made there. Ask each group to make a poster with pictures and information of the cheeses from the country they chose to share with the rest of the class.

Cheese tasting

(Don't let children with dairy intolerance taste cheese.)

Bring in a selection of three or four different kinds of cheese for the children to taste. Choose cheeses that are very different, for example, Cheddar, Lancashire and Stilton.

Label the cheeses and cut up into very small portions.

Wash hands before tasting. Ask the children to taste and say which they like the best, the least. Count how many children like each kind of cheese.

Ask the children to draw a picture of themselves eating a piece of the cheese they like best.

Foreign cheeses

Talk about the many cheeses that are made in different parts of the world. Explain about blue cheeses and soft runny French cheeses as well as hard cheeses such as Gruyere and Emmental. Ask children if they have these kinds of cheese at home. Do they like them? Ask older children to look at maps to find out where these foreign cheeses are made. Can they draw a map of Europe and label the areas where different cheeses are made?

How is cheese made?

Explain that cheese is usually made from cow's milk that has gone sour. Other kinds of cheeses are made from goat's milk, sheep's milk or buffalo milk.

Ask younger children to draw a wedge of cheese in the middle of the paper and to draw a cow, a sheep and a goat around their picture of the cheese. Help them to write the names of the animals.

Ask older children to investigate these 'non cow' cheeses. They can get information from books or the internet using search engines.

Picnic hampers

Talk to the children about a picnic hamper. Explain that these were once used by many people when they went on picnics and were usually made of wicker which comes from thin branches of trees

Willow trees would be coppiced – that is cut down to the ground so that new bendy branches would grow. These branches were woven to make baskets.

Explain to the children how the pieces of wicker were woven in and out. Use strips of paper or ribbon and show how weaving them can make a plate or container. In craft work help the children to make a woven mat from strips of paper, tape or ribbon. (You can use this later in the celebration section.)

Modern picnic containers

Talk about the kinds of containers we use when we want to keep food safe, clean and whole. Plastic containers are often used these days instead of paper. Talk about the children's lunch boxes that keep their lunches clean and separate. These would be useful for picnics. Ask the children to draw or design a suitable picnic box that would hold salad, fruit and a drink for a picnic.

Plastic bags

Remind the children about the need to recycle plastic bags so that they can be made into new bags to be used. Tell them that British shoppers get though eight billion free plastic shopping bags a year. (Can any of the children write that number?) Explain that in some places the plastic bag has become a menace; in the Irish Republic a new law called 'Bag Tax' has been introduced. Retailers must charge for plastic carrier bags to try and minimize the amount of plastic we use in a bid to help the environment.

Do their families recycle bags? Is it easier to throw everything away in the same black bag and let the rubbish men take it? Remind the children about where rubbish goes (see the activity about composting in the Barbecue section). Can they persuade their families to re-use plastic bags and recycle worn ones at their supermarket? Can they design a poster to display to try to persuade people to recycle plastic bags?

Fruits

Ask the children which fruits they would like to have on a picnic. Which need to be peeled and which need to be washed?

Ask the children to help you to make two lists, fruits you peel and fruits you wash. Read through the list of fruits and ask the children to raise a fist if they like each one. Count up the children who like each fruit and put the number alongside. Are there some fruits that everyone likes? That no-one likes? Talk about the fruits that grow in this country both outdoors and in greenhouses. Talk about more exotic fruits that grow in other countries.

Give each child the 'Fruits' activity sheet and ask them all to draw the fruits they like and to write the names alongside.

> **Fruits**
>
> You peel:
> oranges
> tangerines
> melon
> bananas.
>
> You wash:
> apples
> pears
> plums
> peaches
> apricots
> nectarines
> strawberries
> raspberries.

On the other side of the sheet, ask younger children to draw a picture of themselves eating fruit at a picnic; ask older children to write about the fruits they like to eat raw and to say why they like them. Can some of them write about the dishes made from cooking apples and plums that they could take on a picnic?

Remind all the children about 'five a day'.

Cakes and biscuits

Talk about the kinds of cakes you might have on a picnic. Ask the children if they have helped to make cakes at home for a picnic. Ask those who have helped to tell you about the cakes they have made. Would taking biscuits on a picnic be a good idea? What about chocolate biscuits on a hot day? Remind the children about the biscuits they made in the 'teatime' section. Can they remember the ingredients?

Let's make it – cheese

Make sure that you and the children wash hands before this activity.

Remind the children that cheese is made from milk which has been allowed to go sour and turn into curds and whey before the whey is poured off leaving the curd or immature cheese. Bring into the classroom some creamy milk which is not fresh. If you have access to farm fresh milk this will turn into cheese quicker than pasteurised. Put this into a glass jug or bowl and cover it with a cloth. Leave it in a warm place. This should soon begin to turn and there will be some smell. When the mixture has separated into curds and whey, strain the mixture through a muslin cloth, pouring off the whey. Leave the curds to harden, or when it is ready but still soft you could spread it onto bread or crackers to taste.

Let's make it – picnic pizza

Make sure that you and the children wash hands before this activity.

You can use a dough base for pizza, but a simple scone mix will also suffice. Write the recipe on the board.

With clean hands ask the children to measure and weigh the ingredients. Put the flour into a bowl and rub the warm fat into the flour. Add the milk slowly until there is a soft dough. Put the dough onto a floured board and roll it into a circle.

Brush olive oil over the pizza base right to the edges and then spread tomato paste not quite to the edges. Add two or three toppings, such as mushrooms, sliced tomatoes (or tinned tomatoes drained and chopped), small cubes of ham or cooked bacon, cubes of courgette, black olives and anchovies. Finish by sprinkling 1 teaspoon of oregano or basil and grated cheese over the top. Cook in a hot oven for 15 – 20 minutes. Cut up, share and enjoy.

Pizza base, scone mix

225 grams self-raising flour
40 grams butter or margarine at room temperature
5 fl oz milk
flour for rolling.

Toppings

You'll need:

* tomato paste
* tsp oregano or basil
* grated cheese

Plus selection of:

* cubed tomatoes
* mushrooms
* cubes of ham/bacon
* courgettes
* olives.

Let's grow it – tomatoes

Show the children the seeds in a ripe tomato and explain that in these seeds is all that is needed to grow new plants. Separate the seeds from the flesh and dry them off with some tissue. Plant several of them in some potting compost in a seed tray; water, put on a sunny windowsill and wait... Record the development of the plants and when flowers appear, nudge the pot a bit to allow the pollen to fly about. When the fruits ripen, wash them and share them among the children. You could put them in a sandwich or wrap.

Tomatoes usually ripen in late summer when some schools may be on holiday so why not ask children to take them home to care for during the holiday. If you have a school garden plot you could plant them out and ask the caretaker or a friend to give them water during dry weather.

Let's reflect and share

Remind the children that they have been learning about picnic foods. Can they tell you what a balanced picnic meal would be? Do some of them have picnics and help to get the food ready?

Ask children to share this learning with their families at home by taking the pizza recipe home with pictures of themselves enjoying a picnic.

Ask older children to write a fact sheet about really healthy picnic foods and 'treat' picnic foods.

Remind them that no food is bad for them, but that some foods are healthier for them than others and that some foods that are not quite so healthy can be used as treats. Remind them that 'fresh is best' and about the 'five a day rule'.

Fruits

My name is

Draw some fruits and write their names.

Fruits you peel:	Fruits you wash:
Fruits grown in this country:	**Fruits grown in other countries:**

Section 7: Parties and Celebrations

In this section the children will be thinking about the foods and drink we have at parties or celebrations.

Let's make it – smoothies

You'll need various ingredients from the recipe on page 109.

Let's make it – jellies

You'll need

- gelatine
- a jelly mould
- orange or other juice
- a kettle.

Let's make it – vegetable dips

You'll need

- a carrot

  a pepper
- a courgette
- some celery
- an avocado
- a small amount of dressing from page 85.

Let's make it – celebration cake

See list of ingredients on page 110.

Let's make it – cup cakes

See list of ingredients on page 111.

Suggested letter to parents and carers before starting work on this section

Dear Parents and Carers

Parties and Celebrations

As part of our work on balanced eating we will be learning about and doing activities about the food and drink we eat on special occasions, at parties or celebrations. We will be finding out about both healthy foods and party 'treats'.

We will be making milk smoothies, jellies and cakes and vegetable dips as well as a celebration cake.

We hope that you will show your child that you are interested in this work and support them while they are doing this project. If your child has any special dietary needs please make sure we know about them before we start.

Yours sincerely,

Parties and Celebrations

The way in...

In Circle Time start by talking about a party you have been to. Tell the children about the occasion and the things you did there. Talk about the things you ate and drank there. Explain that this section is all about party and celebration food and that you will have to decide what the party is for – what are you celebrating?

Perhaps you can celebrate the end of a term, the completion of some work or some other school celebration, such as the school's birthday. Who will you invite? Talk about this to set the scene.

Talk about the things you do at parties. Will you have games? Will you have music? Will some children, or someone else, entertain the class?

> **At parties we...**
>
> play games
> have music games
> dress up
> have entertainers
> have balloons
> eat party food
> have party drinks
> have ice cream
> eat jellies
> have a party cake
> light candles.

Ask the children to finish the sentence: 'At parties we eat...' Jot down on the board what the children say to make a list. When all the children have finished, read the list to them and talk about the foods. Which will you have at your party? Can you all make the special cake?

Before ending the Circle Time session ask the children to close their eyes and think of a party they have had at home. Ask them to make a picture in their heads of the people and what they did at the party and tell them that you will want them to draw this picture later.

Homework

Ask the children to start to collect and bring in empty packets that have contained crisps and nibbles, salty biscuits, nuts, pretzels, cheese balls and other snack foods. They can also collect tins and bottles of the drink that they have at parties.

Younger Children

Draw and Talk

Ask the children to remember the picture they made in their heads about a party at home. Ask them to draw a picture of this party with all the people there enjoying themselves.

As the children finish their pictures ask them to come to you (or the classroom helper) in a quiet place to talk about their picture. As each child tells you about their picture write keywords of foods in a corner of the picture.

Ask each child these three prompt questions:

1. What else do you like to eat at parties?

2. What do you like to drink at parties?

3. Which of these foods are 'treats' and which are healthy foods, helping you to grow up fit and healthy?

Take the drawings to the next Circle Time and ask the children if you can show their pictures to everyone and read out the things they have said.

Talk about the most popular foods and make a list of them. Are these all the 'treat' foods?

Make a list of the other foods. Are these all the healthy foods?

Talk about which foods are treats and which are healthy foods. Draw a green ring around the healthy foods.

My party

sandwiches

sausages

crisps

salty biscuits

chocolate biscuits

jelly

ice cream

cakes

fizzy drink.

Biscuits and crisps are treats, so are jelly and ice cream. Fizzy drinks are treats. Sandwiches and sausages can be healthy foods.

Make sure that the children realise that treats are really OK and that we all like treats, especially at parties, but that if we only ever eat 'treat' foods our bodies will not grow up to be healthy bodies and we can be unhealthy as we get older.

Talk about the drinks they have drawn and remind the children that fizzy drinks are OK for treats but that if they only ever drink fizzy drinks, and never drink water, their bodies may become unhealthy as they get older.

Start your class picture about celebrations, adding to it as you work through this section.

Older Children

Draw and Write

Explain the rules for Draw and Write, to use their own ideas without sharing them and without talking about what they are drawing. Remind them to be ready to stop drawing and start the writing when asked and:

- not to worry about spellings

- to ask the scribe in a whisper to write what they say if they need help

- to go back to finish their drawing when they have written all they can.

Ask the children to think about the picture they made in their heads in Circle Time – a party at home. Then ask them to fold their paper in half and on the top half to draw this picture of two plates – a dinner and a pudding – and a drink. After the children have had a few minutes to draw, stop them and ask them to write on the other half of the paper about:

- who is at the party

- the food at the party

- what there is to drink at the party

- whether the food and drink is healthy or all 'treat' food and drink.

All my family is at the party. We are having it in the garden because there isn't room indoors. We will have sandwiches and cakes and my mum's special Pavlova. There will be squash and wine to drink.

Some sandwiches and cakes are healthy but not Pavlova; that's a treat we only have at parties.

When all the children have finished their drawing and writing, ask them to join you in a group or circle to talk about what they have drawn and written and their feelings about party food.

Have the children only drawn 'treat' foods? Jot these down in a list.

What healthy foods have they drawn? Jot these down in a list. Are there any salads or fruit? Which do the children think are the healthiest? Which are not so healthy?

Can any of the children think of healthy substitutes that are still fun and interesting to replace some of the 'treat' foods and drinks?

Start your class picture about celebrations, adding to it as you work through this section.

Activities

We love celebrating

Ask the children to think of all the parties and celebrations they have been to. Make a list of these. Do they wear special clothes to any of these? Do they stay up late for any of these celebrations? Are they annual events or just one special occasion?

Ask the younger children to draw themselves at a celebration and to write a sentence about it underneath their picture.

Ask older children to describe the celebration, writing where it was, why they were celebrating and the people who were there.

Ask them to draw a picture of themselves and other people dressed up at the celebration. You could add some of this work around the class picture you are making, or ask the children to cut out some of their people for the picture.

My sister's wedding

I was a bridesmaid and my dress was blue. I had flowers. The party was good. We had lots of interesting food to eat with our fingers. I tasted some special fizzy drink.

A party table

Remind the children that at a party the table is usually decorated in a special way. Ask the children to tell you what they think will be on a Christmas party table as well as food. They may suggest things such as a fancy cloth, crackers, balloons, presents, flowers, holly, decorations and candles.

Ask children to draw a party table for a birthday party for a six year old boy. Ask them to draw a really good cake, decorations and some presents as well as the food. Ask older children to describe the table and what is on it. They must make sure it is appropriate for a six year old.

Invitations

When you have decided the occasion, you will have to set the date and think about sending out invitations. Write on the board any special words you will need and help the children to know what to

INVITATION

'Come and join our celebration. It's our very special date. We are having a big party. Come along and don't be late!'

say. Help younger children to write a class poem as an invitation! Ask older children to work in pairs to write one.

A fancy dress party

Talk with the children about fancy dress parties. Ask them to finish the sentence: 'At a fancy dress party I would like to be...'

Ask volunteers to talk about what they would wear to be this character. Ask the children to draw themselves dressed in this fancy dress and to write its name. Ask older children to describe the costume and write about how they would feel wearing it.

A surprise party

Ask the children if they have ever been to a surprise party. That's the kind of party where the special guests don't know anything about it.

Talk about how you could organise such a party without them finding out. How would you get the room ready? How would you get the food ready? How would you make sure the person was dressed up and not in their old clothes?

Ask the children to help you to make a list of all the things you would have to do to keep this a secret. Ask older children to write their own list and to make a list of the food and drink they would get ready.

Party food – crisps and things

Ask the children to bring to Circle Time all the packets they have been collecting that have contained crisps and nibbles, salty biscuits and things like that – the kinds of things that you have at parties that are not very healthy but great for treats. Ask each child to say what one of their packets had in it. Ask others who brought the same packets to stand and show theirs.

Lay out on a table one of each kind of packet and either write a number on each or put a card number nearby so that you can identify them. Ask the children to look at all the packets and to write down the numbers of the ones they really like. Collect their paper and add up the numbers so that you find out how many children really like each packet.

Help younger children to read the ingredients of these packets. Help them to find out the salt and fat contents of each and to write this down on the board against the number you have given each packet. Talk about which are the saltiest and which have the most fat. Can they find the healthiest?

Ask older children to make a chart of the contents of as many packets as possible in the time you allow. Can someone collect all these and make one large chart on the computer. Look at which of these 'not so healthy' snacks are the best and which are the worst. You could make a wall display using the packets and the data you have generated.

Drinks – cans and individual bottles

Get out all the (non alcoholic!) drinks bottles and cans that the children have brought in. Set them out on a table so that you can see them easily.

Number each bottle with a permanent marker but make sure you don't cover up the contents information. Put numbered cards down so that each bottle has its own place.

Ask the children to look at the bottles and cans and decide which they like the best. Identify places in the room where children can stand to 'vote with their feet' and count which drinks are most liked. How many chose the water bottle?

For younger children read out the contents of each bottle and ask your Teaching Assistant to write the amount of the sugar and caffeine (if any) on the board against the number of the can to make a chart. Ask children to think which is the healthiest of these drinks and which the least healthy. Have they chosen the ones with the least sugar and caffeine? Would they choose the healthier option now they know?

Ask older children to do their own investigation of the bottles as they have done in previous work. After all the data has been collected and talked about, ask the children how many of them would choose to drink the healthier option.

Drinks – squashes

Ask the children to do the same activities with the empty bottles of squash and other drinks that have to be diluted, for example, blackcurrant, lemon barley, orange, lime. Ask the children which drinks they think are the healthiest, apart from water, the ones in cans and individual bottles or the ones that you dilute with water.

The children can use the activity sheet, 'Fruit squash drinks', to record their findings. Ask them to draw a circle around the words that best describe how well they like each drink.

Can they decide which is the healthiest one, that's the one with the least sugar and most fruit?

Let's make it – dairy free fruit smoothies

You could use either of these recipes or use your own.

Ingredients:	Ingredients:
1 banana ½ cup frozen strawberries about 1 cup water 4 tbs orange or pineapple juice.	1 ½ cups of vanilla-flavoured soya milk ½ to ¾ cup frozen berries (any kind) 1 teaspoon honey.

Mash up the fruit until it is really soft, put it in the blender and add liquid. Share among the children and enjoy.

Experiment by using other fruits such as raspberries, pears and kiwi fruit.

Let's make it – jellies

NB Children who are vegetarians may not have gelatine unless it is the vegetarian kind.

Make sure that you and the children wash hands before this activity.

You'll need gelatine, a jelly mould, orange or other juice, a kettle.

Ask the children to stand up, turn around and sit down if they like jelly. Ask them if anyone can tell the class how to make jelly. They will probably tell you about commercially produced jellies that you buy and melt in hot water. Praise them for their explanation.

Explain that you can make jellies out of gelatine and fruit juice. Talk about these being fun to make and healthy to eat.

Boil some water and melt the gelatine according to the instructions on the pack. Add the fruit juice instead of water to make up slightly less than the required amount. Let all the children stir the mixture and sniff the aroma. Pour it into the mould(s) or a dish and allow to set. You can add fruit to the jelly, if you do, reduce the amount of liquid to aid setting.

Let's make it – vegetable dips

Make sure that you and the children wash hands before this activity.

You will need a carrot, pepper, courgette, celery, avocado, small amount of dressing from page 77.

Make avocado dip by mashing up the avocado and adding a small amount of the salad dressing. Pour into small dish.

Peel the carrot, wash the celery and courgette. Cut them all into thin sticks.

Serve the vegetables with the dip.

Let's make it – celebration cake

Make sure that you and the children wash hands before this activity.

Tell the children that you are going to make a celebration sponge cake with a creamy filling and icing. If you make more than one, you could use a chocolate mixture for the second, by adding some cocoa in place of some of the flour. They could also melt real chocolate to make the icing.

If your class has four main groups, you could help two groups to make the cakes and two to make the cup cakes below.

You will need a mixing bowl, two large sandwich tins to cook it in and these ingredients:

- 3 eggs
- their weight in sifted self-raising flour
- their weight in soft margarine
- their weight in sugar.

To decorate:

- 400 gm. icing sugar
- 50 gm. soft margarine
- little milk, water, fruit juice
- decorations, such as hundreds and thousands, silver balls, icing flowers.

Show the children how to grease and flour the tins.

Help them to mix the sugar and fat together until it is soft and fluffy. Let them crack the eggs and beat them one at a time. Show them how to add the eggs with a little flour to the sugar and butter mixture and beat it all together. Fold in the flour carefully.

Put half the mixture in one tin and half in the other, smoothing it down until it is level. Put these into a moderate oven or ask the school cook to do this for you, allowing the children into the kitchen to smell the mixture as it cooks.

Help the children to turn out the cooled cakes carefully.

To decorate, soften the margarine, add half the icing sugar and mix, add enough liquid for a spreading consistency. Help the children to spread this onto one of the cakes and put the other on top of it. Mix the rest of the icing sugar with a very little liquid and spread it over the top layer. Add decorations.

Let's make it – cup cakes

Make sure that you and the children wash hands before this activity.

You will need:

- the same ingredients as for the cake or if less, use only two eggs
- 200 grams icing sugar (or melted chocolate) for the topping
- some flavourings and pink or red colouring
- some very small paper cases – those for petit fours are best.

Mix by the same method as for the cake, adding colouring to half the mixture. Put a teaspoon into each small paper case and cook for about 10 minutes.

Cover each cup cake with icing and add a decoration.

Let's reflect and share

Organise a party for your class, using some of the foods they have made in this and other sections. Send out invitations to people who have helped them and arrange the classroom as a party venue. Use the woven paper mats the children made (page 96) as plates or make new mats out of A4 paper decorated by the children. Help them to make paper hats from sugar paper or decorated newspaper.

Enjoy your celebration!

Remind the children that they have been learning about 'treat' foods we eat at parties or on special occasions. Remind them that these treats are OK to eat on these special occasions, but not to eat every day.

Ask younger children to draw the party foods and drinks they have helped to make so that they can take these pictures home to share with their families.

Ask older children to write out the recipes to take home. Perhaps their families will let them make some of these at home.

If this is your final piece of work with these children, celebrate their learning and praise them for their new understanding about foods that will help them to stay healthy and have healthy bodies when they grow up.

Remind them again that no food is bad for them, but that some foods are healthier for them than others and that some foods that are not quite so healthy can be used as treats.

Fruit Squash Drinks   My name is ....

Name of squash ………….………………………………....

Name of fruits in squash ……………………..………….....

Dilute with one part squash to ………...…. parts of water

Amount of fruit as percentage …………….….................

What else is in the squash? ....

....

....…......

....…......

I liked this squash   **a lot**   **a bit**   **not very much**   **not at all**

drawing of bottle

Name of squash …………….…………………………….....

Name of fruits in squash ……………………..…………....

Dilute with one part squash to ………...…. parts of water

Amount of fruit as percentage …………….…..................

What else is in the squash? ....

....

....…......

....…......

I liked this squash   **a lot**   **a bit**   **not very much**   **not at all**

drawing of bottle

Turn over the page and draw yourself drinking your favourite drink. What is it? Why do you like it?

Let's celebrate and spread the word

Talk to the children about all that they now know about healthy foods and drinks. Ask each child to draw and label or draw and write all they can remember about the foods and drinks that go to make balanced eating. Ask them to make a display for all the school to share.

Ask each child to make a food triangle to add to the display. Use the Pyramid of Foods for younger children to use to draw in the levels of foods in a balanced diet. Older children can draw their own equilateral triangle using a ruler and a pair of compasses and draw the levels showing the amounts of the six groups of foods that go to make a suggested balanced diet. Ask them to write examples of the foods in these six groups. Ask the children to complete the activity sheet 'What I ate yesterday!' and display some of these.

Invite parents to come to see this display and hand out any fact sheets that you think would interest them. You might like to make a large triangle of a balanced diet to put on display for parents to read.

You could make this your celebration for all the work in this book by providing healthy foods and drinks for your guests.

Healthy eating means eating lots of different kinds of foods to keep your body healthy.

Can you draw the foods in the triangle?

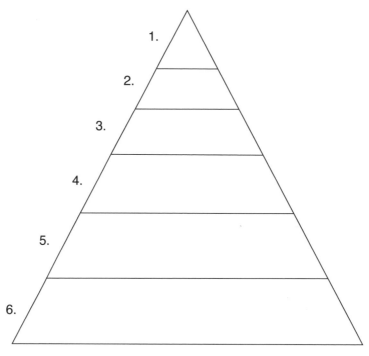

1. Fats, oils, sugar.
Crisps, chocolate, biscuits, cakes.
Eat little of these foods.

2. Meat, poultry, fish, eggs and pulses
Protein to help you grow and keep you healthy.
2-3 protions of these each day.

3. Milk, yoghurt and cheese
Calcium and protein for bones, teeth and brain.
2-3 portions of these each day.

4. Fruit
Vitamins, helps to fight germs.
Eat 2 to 4 portions of these each day.

5. Vegetables, vitamins and special things to make and keep you well.
3-5 portions each day.

6. Bread, rice, pasta, creral give you energy.
6-11 portions each day.

What I Ate Yesterday My name is _____

Think back to yesterday and the food you ate.

Draw or write about the portions you had of these foods.

Fruit	Vegetables
Eggs	**Meat**
Sugar	**Fat**
Milk	**Water**

Would yesterday's food make a good triangle? Yes ☺ No ☹

Turn over. Draw yourself eating your favourite not treat food. Write about it.

Appendix

Some Useful Books and Websites

Bull, Jane (2002) *The Cooking Book*, Dorling Kindersley.
Interesting ideas and recipes for fun food to make at school and home.

Chambers, Catherine (1996) *Grasses*, Evans, London.
This book gives interesting information about different kinds of grasses, what we get from them and what we can do with them.

Gibson, Ray (1990) *Kitchen Fun* from the 'You and Your child' series, Usborne, London
Lots of fun ideas for children to make interesting foods.

Robinson, Sally (2005) *Healthy Eating in Primary Schools*, London: Paul Chapman Publishing/ A Lucky Duck Book.

Smith, Kathryn (Editor) (1992) *Food Facts Additives*, Wayland.
For teachers and older children, full of facts about additives old and new.

Stoppard, Miriam (1992) *First Food Made Fun*, Dorling Kindersley, London.
Though this book is intended for babies and toddlers it has great ideas for presenting foods in an interesting and fun way. There are recipes too.

Steer, Gina (1995) *Burgers and Hot Dogs*, Quintet Publishing, London.
Wonderful ways for healthy burgers and hot dogs.

Woolfitt, Gabrielle (1994) *What's Cooking?* Wayland Publishers Ltd., Hove, UK.
Mainly for Key Stage 2 and older, this book has healthy ideas and recipes as well as some food science.

Websites

http://www.health-alliance.com/nn/hheguide/intro_3.html guide to heart healthy eating

http://www.health24.com/dietnfood/Water_centre/15-167-166.asp
Information on: water, diet and nutrition, water and children, water and your body.

http://www.hdra.org.uk/ for information about organics

For a healthy living plate of food with explanations of portion size, visit website:
http://www.healthyliving.gov.uk/healthyeating/index.cfm?contentid=1465

For information about recycling visit: www.greenchoices.org/recycling.html

http://www.teachernet.gov.uk/growingschools/

Jamie Oliver's website is: http://www.jamieoliver.net

Fact Sheet: The School Fruit and Vegetable Scheme

The School Fruit and Vegetable Scheme is part of the 5 A DAY programme to increase fruit and vegetable consumption.

Under the Scheme, all four to six year old children in LEA maintained infant, primary and special schools will be entitled to a free piece of fruit or vegetable each school day. It was introduced after the NHS Plan 2000 included a commitment to implement a national school fruit scheme by 2004.

Following the success of the early pilots, £42million from the New Opportunities Fund, the largest of the lottery good cause distributors, has been supporting the expansion of the scheme region by region. By April 2004, the scheme was available in the West Midlands, London, the North West, the East Midlands and the North East, covering one million children. The Department of Health in January 2004 announced it would take over funding, at a cost of £77million over the next two years. The remaining regions of South East, South West, Yorkshire & the Humber, and East of England will join the scheme in Autumn Term 2004.

In September carrots and tomatoes were added to apples, pears, bananas & easy-peel citrus, and so the Scheme's name has changed to the School Fruit and Vegetable Scheme.

This information and more from the following website:

http://www.5aday.nhs.uk

Fact Sheet: Hens and Eggs

Abridged from www.vegsoc.org/info/laying.html

There are over 33 million laying hens in the UK.

About 85% are kept in battery cages.

Alternatives systems are percheries (aviaries) and free-range systems.

Only about 10% of laying hens in the UK are free-range but this is likely to increase.

Battery hens

Cages are arranged in rows of three to six tiers inside huge sheds without windows. There can be as many as 30,000 birds in one shed. Heating, ventilation and lighting are all automatically controlled. Egg-laying is promoted by light and so artificial lighting is kept on for 17 hours a day to help increase production. Feeding and watering is also automated and can contain animal products and growth promoting antibiotics, yolk colourings and additives.

Percheries

The hens are kept in large windowless sheds with several rows of perches at different heights. The floor will be partly covered with litter (wood shavings or straw) and nest boxes are provided. Percheries are often old battery sheds that have been converted. Eggs from percheries are called barn eggs.

Free-range

About three million hens are free-range. Traditional free-range involves smaller flocks which are housed in moveable houses in fields with access to the open air where they can peck for additional food.

Sadly, 10% of these are commercial systems with massive flocks in huge sheds. These hens must have access through holes to open-air runs with not more than 1,000 birds per hectare.

Fact Sheet: Salt

For more information visit http://www.davidgregory.org/salt.htm

The amount of salt we consume depends on our individual eating habits, but typically about 20 per cent of our salt intake is from foods that naturally contain salt, such as eggs, meat and fish.

At the table, a typical person adds an estimated 15 per cent of his or her intake to food. The remainder of the salt in our diet is added during cooking or comes from processed foods.

Many foods contribute to total salt intake without being perceived as being salty. For example, white bread and cornflakes both contain salt but, unlike potato crisps or nuts, the salt is contained within the food and not on the surface, where it is more easily detected.

In the UK White Paper 'Saving Lives: Our Healthier Nation' (1999) the UK Government affirmed a commitment to explore the scope for reducing the salt content of processed foods as part of its action to reduce the death rate from cardiovascular disease (CVD). The US authorities recommend limiting sodium intake to 100 mmol (2.4 g/day) equivalent to 6 g salt/day.

The British Heart Foundation suggests a lower limit of 1.6 g salt a day and an upper limit of 6 g, and calls for more informative food labelling.

The UK Food Standards Agency (May 2003) has, for the first time, issued salt intake targets to which children's salt consumption should be reduced. The advice is based on the SACN Report. Recommendations are made on the 'Daily target average salt intakes' for children, according to their age. The new advice recommends:

- for children aged 0-6 months, the aim should be less than 1 gram a day
- 7-12 months, 1 gram/day
- 1-3 years, 2 grams/day
- 4-6 years, 3 grams/day
- 7-10 years, 5 grams/day
- 11-14 years, 6 grams/day.

The levels of current average intake for children of four and above are almost certainly higher than these targets. Children's salt consumption is relatively higher than that of adults for their weight.

For more information, see website:
http://www.ifst.org/hottop17.htm

Fact Sheet: Fats

From http://www.health-alliance.com/nn/hheguide/intro_4.html

There are two important aspects to the fat in our diets. One is the quantity of fat and the other is the quality of the fat. Small amounts of some fats are beneficial. The chart below shows how some of the fats are categorized.

Monounsaturated fats come from plant sources. They are usually liquid at room temperature. Overall, these fats tend to lower total cholesterol and low-density lipoproteins (LDL) in the blood. They help to maintain or slightly raise high-density lipoprotein (HDL).

Polyunsaturated fats are also from plant sources. They are usually liquid at room temperature. Their overall effect is to lower total cholesterol and LDL in the blood. They may also slightly lower HDL.

Dietary cholesterol is present in all foods of animal origin such as meat, fish, poultry, egg yolks and high fat dairy products. There is no cholesterol in vegetables, fruits, nuts or grains. Dietary cholesterol has less effect on raising and lowering blood cholesterol than the saturated fat does.

Saturated fats are found in foods of animal origin (meat, fish, poultry and high fat dairy products). They are also present in palm oil, palm kernel oil, coconut oil, cocoa butter and hydrogenated vegetable oils. They are usually solid at room temperature. Saturated fats raise total blood cholesterol, particularly LDL.

Hydrogenated fats are liquid oils processed to a solid form, such as vegetable shortening. They give processed foods a longer shelf life. Although they are made from vegetable oil, the process results in the formation of trans fatty acids that are thought to be as harmful as animal fats. Foods made with fully hydrogenated fats should be avoided.

Partially hydrogenated fats are liquid oils processed to a somewhat solid form. Margarines and many processed foods such as crackers, cookies and convenience mixes are made with partially hydrogenated oils. Usually, the degree of hydrogenation is unknown. Foods containing partially hydrogenated fats should be limited.

Fact Sheet: How a Change in Diet Can Help Lower Blood Cholesterol

A diet high in total fat and saturated fat can contribute to high levels of cholesterol in your blood. Reducing total fat in your diet will help lower your blood cholesterol. Replacing the saturated fat with moderate amounts of unsaturated fat can lower the bad cholesterol or low-density lipoproteins (LDL) and may slightly raise good cholesterol or high-density lipoprotein (HDL) levels.

A low fat diet

Choose lean, protein-rich foods – soy, fish, skinless chicken, very lean meat, and fat free or 1% dairy products.

Eat foods that are naturally low in fat – like whole grains, fruits, and vegetables.

Get plenty of soluble fibre – with oats, bran, dry peas, beans, cereal, and rice.

Limit your consumption of fried foods, processed foods, and commercially prepared baked goods (donuts, cookies, crackers).

Limit animal products such as egg yolks, cheeses, whole milk, cream, ice cream, and fatty meats (and large portions of meats).

Look at food labels, especially for the level of saturated fat. Avoid or limit foods high in saturated fat (more than 20% on the label).

Look on food labels for words such as 'hydrogenated' or 'partially hydrogenated' – these foods are loaded with saturated fats and trans-fatty acids and should be avoided.

Liquid vegetable oil, soft margarine and trans fatty acid-free margarine are preferable to butter, stick margarine or shortening.

Fact Sheet: Five Portions of Fruit or Veg a Day

What is a portion?

One glass of fruit juice (however many you have, it is still one portion)
one apple, pear, banana, orange, nectarine or peach
one slice of melon
half an avocado or grapefruit
two plums; a large piece of cucumber
an 80g portion of cauliflower or broccoli
one tomato, pepper or a large onion.

Three heaped tablespoons of any vegetable, for example, peas, carrots, sweetcorn.
Three heaped tablespoons of beans or pulses.

For more information about portion sizes see the following website:
http://www.5aday.nhs.uk and click on the 'What counts as a portion?' link.

As part of a healthy balanced diet we are recommended to eat at least five portions of a variety of fruit and veg each day, whether they are fresh, frozen, canned, dried or juiced (but fruit juice only counts as a maximum of one portion a day). Dried fruit such as currants, sultanas, raisins, dates and figs provide energy in the form of sugar and are a good source of fibre. They also contain other vitamins and minerals, but not vitamin C, which is found in fresh fruit. A portion of dried fruit is one heaped tablespoon. This is less than a portion of fresh fruit because it's based on the equivalent weight of fresh fruit.

From http://www.eatwell.gov.uk/healthydiet/foodmyths/

What about tinned and frozen fruit and vegetables?

Modern freezing preserves the healthy ingredients so frozen fruit and vegetables can be better than fresh produce that has been left out at room temperature for a long time.

Tinned vegetables and fruit, and dried fruit such as raisins, are also acceptable.

How can we increase our daily intake?

It's a good idea to:

- have a bowl of fruit set out to make it easy to get an apple, orange or pear

- never serve a meal without including at least one vegetable or piece of fruit.

More information from the following websites:
http://www.5aday.nhs.uk (click on the 'Health Professionals' link on the home page)
http://www.thinkvegetables.co.uk invites you to download images of up to 35 different vegetables.

Fact Sheet: Caffeine

Caffeine is a mild stimulant that occurs naturally in coffee and cocoa beans, tea leaves and kola nuts (the basic ingredient in colas).

Too much caffeine can elevate your heart rate and make you anxious for a few hours until the drug has had a chance to work its way out of your system, although people who take caffeine regularly are generally less sensitive to its effects.

This buzz may keep you awake at night, but it won't sober you up if you've been drinking.

Caffeine also stimulates the flow of stomach acid, so it may aggravate ulcers.

Experts disagree whether it is addictive, but many studies show that caffeine junkies do experience withdrawal symptoms, including headaches, drowsiness and a lack of concentration, when they miss their fix.

Children can get hooked too. One study found that 8 to 12-year-olds who had been getting the equivalent of three cans of cola a day had shorter attention spans for a week when their caffeine supply was taken away. Cutting back gradually can help you avoid symptoms.

Many medications, including some pain relievers, cold and allergy remedies, and appetite-control pills, contain caffeine as well.

The important point to remember is that caffeine, like many other substances, is not harmful when taken in moderation. However, if taken to excess, then it may cause problems in some people. For more information visit http://nootropics. com/caffeine/faq.html

Sources of caffeine

The richest sources of caffeine are tea, coffee, cola drinks, some over-the-counter medications, chocolate and cocoa.

As little as 20 mgs of caffeine can produce noticeable body and mood changes. As a rough guide to how much caffeine you may be taking on a daily basis...

- An average cup of tea contains around 60 mgs of caffeine.

- A cup of instant coffee contains over 100 mgs. Instant decaffeinated coffee contains about 3 mgs.

- Brewed coffee can contain 25-50% more caffeine than instant. Espresso coffee can have a higher concentration of caffeine and it is assimilated more quickly.

- A 12 oz can of regular or diet cola contains between 35 and 45 mgs. of caffeine depending on the brand.

- One ounce of chocolate contains about 15 mgs.

http://www.pe2000.com/caffeine.htm

Fact Sheet: Sugar

Visit http://www.sucrose.com/lhist.html

The sugar that is produced from sugar cane is identical to sugar that is derived from the sugar beet.

Sugar cane

Sugar cane grows in tropical and subtropical climates and more than half of the world's supply of sugar comes from sugar cane. Harvesting of cane is often done by machines that top the canes at a uniform height, cut them off at ground level, and deposit them in rows but in Florida it is mainly cut by hand.

Cane sugar is made by grinding the stalks, shredding them through toothed rollers and then boiling the liquid until it is like a thick syrup. As the liquid evaporates crystals are formed. When as much sugar as possible has crystallized in the syrup, the mixture is spun in a centrifuge, which separates it from the remaining syrup (now called molasses). The raw sugar is then dissolved again into crystals of various sizes. It can be made into powdered, granulated and lump sugar as well as brown sugars, which contain some molasses.

The remaining molasses is not wasted but used to make ethanol and rum, as a table syrup and food flavouring, as food for farm animals, and in the manufacture of several processed tobaccos.

Sugar beet

Sugar beet is a kind of beetroot, a member of the goosefoot family and is grown in a temperate climate. Sugar beet is the chief source of sugar for most of Europe and is grown extensively in Europe (Russia, Ukraine, Germany, France, and Poland). About two-fifths of all sugar is made from sugar beet.

After the leaves and tops have been removed, the roots are cut into chips at the sugar factory. These are then crushed to remove the juice. The juice is processed, refined and bleached to produce sugar. It is processed similar to sugar production from sugar cane. The pulp that remains is used as food for animals. Beet molasses is fed to livestock.

The sugars found naturally in whole fruit are less likely to cause tooth decay because the sugar is contained within the structure of the fruit. But, when fruit is juiced or blended, the sugar is released. Once released, these sugars can damage teeth, especially if fruit juice is drunk frequently.

But fruit juice is still a healthy choice. One glass (150ml) counts as one of the five fruit and veg portions we should all be aiming for each day.

To help keep teeth healthy, it's best to have fruit juice at mealtimes, particularly for children. Milk or water are good choices for children to drink between meals. http://www.eatwell.gov.uk/healthydiet/foodmyths/

Fact Sheet: Chocolate

See http://www.chocolate.org/

This is made from the fruits of the cacao tree (cocoa beans). Cacao beans were used by the Aztecs in South America to prepare to a hot, frothy beverage with stimulant and restorative properties. Chocolate itself was reserved for warriors, nobility and priests. The Aztecs esteemed its reputed ability to confer wisdom and vitality.

In 1519 the Spanish adventurer Hernán Cortés was given a hot chocolate drink made from cocoa beans by Aztecs. Cortés took it back to Spain and it spread through Europe as a drink.

It was not until 1847 that the first 'chocolate for eating' was produced by Fry and Sons of Bristol.

The first milk chocolate, prepared by adding powdered milk to the pressed cocoa bean, was produced in Switzerland in 1875.

The first step in chocolate-making is to harvest ripe pods of cocoa beans; these are split to release the beans which are fermented in heaps or boxes for about a week before being dried for export.

In the chocolate factory, the beans are roasted, broken down into small pieces and the shells are removed. The cocoa bits are ground to form chocolate mass – a thick liquid that solidifies on cooling.

This is then mixed with additional cocoa butter (extracted in the manufacture of cocoa powder), sugar and vanilla. Milk is then added to make milk chocolate.

In the United Kingdom up to 5 per cent vegetable oil is added, to compensate for variations in cocoa butter and to ensure that the texture is consistent.

In most other European countries no vegetable oil is added in the manufacture of chocolate. The mixture is then mixed, and carefully beaten to make sure that the fat and sugar crystallize in a stable form.

Chocolate is source of energy with only a small amount of nutrients, a little iron, a lot of fat and sugar.

Fact Sheet: Reasons to go Organic

© Ysanne Spevack – adapted from the Organicfood.co.uk website http://www.organicfood.co.uk/topten.html

Organic produce is not covered in poisonous chemicals. The average apple has 20-30 artificial poisons on its skin, even after rinsing. Trust your instincts and go organic!

Fresh organic produce contains on average 50% more vitamins, minerals, enzymes and other micro-nutrients than intensively farmed produce. Science says that it's good for you.

Going organic is the only practical way to avoid eating genetically modified (GM) food.

If you eat dairy or meat products, going organic has never been more essential to safeguard you and your family's health. Intensively-reared dairy cows and farm animals are fed antibiotics, hormones, anti-parasite drugs and other medicines on a daily basis, whether they are ill or not.

About 99% of non-organic farm animals in the UK are now fed GM soya. Common sense says that organic is safe food.

Organic produce simply tastes so much better. Fruit and vegetables full of juice and flavour, and so many different varieties to try! There are about 100 different kinds of organic potatoes in production in the UK, and that's just potatoes!

Organic farms support and nurture our beautiful and diverse wildlife. Over the last thirty years, intensive farming in the UK has led to dramatic erosion of the soil, a fall of up to 70% of wild birds in some areas, the destruction of ancient hedgerows, and the near extinction of some of the most beautiful species of butterflies, frogs, grass-snakes and wild mammals.

We spend billion of pounds every year cleaning up the mess that agro-chemicals make to our natural water supply. Go organic for a genuine more cost-effective future.

Intensive farming can seriously damage farm workers' health. There are much higher instances of cancer, respiratory problems and other major diseases in farm workers from non-organic farms. This is particularly true in developing countries, and for agrochemical farms growing cotton.

And if you simply like the idea of your children and grandchildren being able to visit the countryside and play in the forests and fields just like we did when we were young, go organic for the sake of all of our futures.

More information from the website: http://www.hdra.org.uk

Fact Sheet: Composting

Why should we compost?

Because:

- 25% of all household waste could be composted

- the finished compost is excellent garden fertilizer and it costs nothing

- making garden and food waste into compost cuts down on the rubbish that has to be transported to landfill sites.

How do I compost?

You'll need some kind of container. You can make one out of wood; it needs closed sides and a lid; a lift out wall section for getting finished compost out is ideal. You'll need to get at the compost to aerate it occasionally.

Most local authorities sell compost bins.

What can I compost?

All organic matter from your kitchen and garden.

Where should I put the bin?

Somewhere within easy reach all year round, preferably on soil which allows earthworms in to aerate the compost.

How does composting actually work?

Organic waste is rotted down through the activity of microbes and bacteria. They need the right levels of moisture and air to work effectively.

Ensure air can reach all the contents of the bin – you may have to turn it or try sticking a garden fork in, pushing back and forth to clear a central vent, every few weeks.

The contents of the compost bin should be moist. You may have to add water from time to time. Keep the lid on to prevent rain making it too wet. The compost will get quite hot and this indicates that the bacteria is working effectively.

When is it ready?

When it looks like crumbly dark soil. Access it through the wall section. If you have a plastic bin, access it through the bottom hatch or simply lift the compost bin off the heap and remove with a shovel. Unfinished compost should go back in. It is better to have two or three bins on the go at the same time. One to fill, one to turn, one to use.

http://www.greenchoices.org/gardening.html#compost

Fact Sheet: Olives and Olive Oil in Greece

For more information visit http://www.olivesetal.co.uk

The first known cultivation of the olive tree worldwide took place in Crete about 3500 BC in early Minoan times. At this time the olive tree was much wilder compared to the tree we know today. After 2000 BC cultivation soon began in mainland Greece and olive oil became part of Greek cooking down through the centuries. The olive tree was a symbol in ancient Greece and olive oil was used for its valuable nutritional quality and also for medical purposes. Between the 7th and 3rd centuries BC ancient philosophers, physicians and historians knew the curative properties of olive oil. This knowledge is being 'rediscovered' today as scientists research why the Mediterranean diet is so healthy.

The symbolic meaning of the olive tree is illustrated by the first Olympic Games, at Olympia in 776 BC, when an olive branch was awarded to the winners to symbolise a truce in any hostilities.

Today, Greece has become the world's most important exporter of quality olive oil. Often, when a child is born, parents plant an olive tree which will grow and develop along with the child. When the child is six and starts school, the olive tree is ready to produce its fruit. The tree will outlive the family and will still be around to be tended by the future generations.

Olives in Corfu are harvested from November until April. Some olives are beaten from the tree with poles and caught in large nets. Other olive farmers now harvest by machine or use trunk and branch shakers. The olives are taken at once to an olive press or they will begin to oxidise and ferment. Thousands of years ago, crushing was done by hand in spherical stone basins. Today olives are crushed by mechanical stainless steel grindstones. It takes five kilos of olives to make one litre of oil. It is the cold press method that enables olive oil to maintain its flavour, colour and nutritional value. Olive oil is the only oil that can be used as soon as it is removed from the fruit.

Did you know?

- Greeks consume more olive oil per head than any other nation.
- The olive oil market in Britain is growing at a rate of 25% per annum.
- Only one tablespoon of olive oil will wipe out the cholesterol raising effects of two eggs.
- 4 or 5 tablespoons of olive oil daily improves the blood profiles of heart attack patients
- 2/3 of a tablespoon of olive oil daily lowers blood pressure in men.
- Olive oil consumption in Britain is 1.3 litres per person per year; in Greece it is 25 litres
- 70% of Greek olive oil production is Extra Virgin Olive Oil.

Fact Sheet: Cheese Making

Milks from different species of mammals (cows, goats, sheep buffalo) can be used to make cheese. Milk consists of protein, fat, lactose, minerals. The process of making cheese is an ancient craft that dates back thousands of years.

Cheese making starts either by natural souring of the milk or by adding a starter culture, together with a coagulant, for example, rennet. This turns the milk into soft curd and when the whey is removed, by straining or running off, a firm curd is left. This cheese is salted, moulded and pressed. Then it is left to ripen and mature.

The quality of cheese varies according to the type of milk used. For example, milk containing high total solids (sheep) increases cheese yields and milk high in fat produces softer cheese. The cheese making process has to be modified in relation to the type of milk used.

Making Cheese from curdled milk

1. Milk is carefully selected to make sure there are no antibiotics or harmful agents that could affect the process.

2. The milk is then heated to destroy any harmful bacteria (i.e. pasteurisation).

3. Special starter cultures are then added to the warm milk and change a very small amount of the milk sugar into lactic acid.

4. This acidifies the milk at a much faster rate and prepares it for the next stage.

5. Rennet (mainly chymosin) is then added to the milk and within a short time a curd is produced.

6. The curd is then cut into small cubes, and heated to start a shrinking process which, with the steady production of lactic acid from the starter cultures, will change it into small rice-sized grains.

7. At some point the curd grains fall to the bottom of the cheese vat, the left-over liquid, which consists of water, milk, sugar and albumen (now called whey) is drained off and the curd grains allowed to mat together to form large slabs of curd.

8. The slabs are then milled, and salt is added to provide flavour and help preserve the cheese. Later it is pressed, and subsequently packed in various sized containers for maturing.

See this website for more about cheese and cheese making:
http://137.195.136.5/SDA/cheese2.html

Fact Sheet: Basket Making

Abridged from www.britishbaskets.co.uk/home

The art of basket-making was developed hundreds of years ago. In Britain oak, hazel and willow provided material for making the strong rigid containers necessary in everyday life. Fences and houses, too, were built from wickerwork or wattles.

Where today we use cardboard, plastic or plywood for packing material, two hundred years ago we would have had to use wickerwork. When people gathered fruit and vegetables from the fields, these were put into baskets.

Wicker was used for packing fish, poultry and dairy produce when they were taken to the town markets.

Materials such as manure or rubble needed baskets; wicker was used for animal muzzles, bird traps and beer strainers. It was also used for travelling trunks, hat boxes and umbrella holders of the well-to-do.

Wherever willows grew there would be wicker workshops nearby. Where growing conditions were really good there would be many basket makers, often within a small area of several villages.

At the beginning of the twentieth century, East Anglia and the East Midlands, the plain of York, Worcestershire, Gloucestershire, Kent, Bedfordshire and the Thames Valley had a fair number of country workshops, mostly making simple agricultural baskets. The largest and most sophisticated workshops were found in the towns of Lancashire, Somerset, Nottinghamshire and Leicestershire. Guilds of basket-makers were formed.

Records show that the Worshipful Company of Basket-makers of the City of London was established before 1469. This company was eventually granted a royal charter by George VI in 1937, but by then its old responsibilities had long since been taken on by the trade unions.